Fixing Ameri

First Edition
Printed and bound in the United States
of America
ISBN-13: 978-0615629469
Library of Congress Control Number:
2012906655

Comments can be made at the
http://joesmyth.org/ blog or on the
Fixing America's Broken Politics page on
Facebook. On Twitter, it's
@JoeSmyth99.

Contents

Dedication

This book is dedicated to our children and grandchildren.

My generation owes you an apology for leaving you with an America that is not as great as the one we inherited from our parents and grandparents. We screwed up.

My hope is that you will be able to restore America's greatness.

Foreword

This book details one citizen's proposed solutions to the major political issues that are dividing our nation and undermining America's greatness.

My goal was to make this an easy read for everybody—even those who don't have much time to spend on politics. I hope you'll find lots of "meat" and not much "fat." Each chapter is designed to stand alone, with cross-references to related chapters for those who wish to dig deeper.

I have made a good-faith effort to attribute quotations accurately, but I haven't done exhaustive academic research. I hope readers will understand that it's the content of the quote that is of primary importance.

No one will agree with all of my solutions, and that's okay. My aim is to at least challenge your views and stimulate your thinking about these issues—instead of being sucked in by the sound bites that have allowed a self-serving political elite to preside over our nation's fall from greatness. I hope you'll find a mix of opinions that you might not find anywhere else, since my own thinking doesn't blindly follow any particular school of thought.

I am a regular citizen. I have never been active in partisan politics. I was privileged to have had an inside look at politics as a journalist, an editorial writer, and an editor—always representing a nonpartisan citizen's perspective. Now, as a father of six and grandfather of twenty, this "Joe Citizen" feels compelled to try to do something about our nation's decline before it is too late.

America is supposed to have a government "of, for, and by" the people. Regular citizens—folks like you and me—should be firmly in control. The common sense, brave hearts, and hard work of regular Americans are what made this country great.

Somehow we have allowed a "political elite"—career politicians, their public relations experts, special interest lobbyists, central planners, bureaucrats, and commentators—to dominate political discourse in this country. These self-appointed experts are making a mess of it! They have overcomplicated government to the point where most of us can't even fill out our own tax returns.

Foreword

I speak out now knowing that some of my opinions will offend left and right, rich and poor, black, brown, white, independents, Democrats, Republicans, Tea Partyers, and Occupy Wall Streeters. If you disagree with some of my stances, all I ask is that you consider the related chapters so you can see how various issues overlap and interrelate.

My opinions are just that: one citizen's opinions. I'm honored that you're willing to consider mine, but make sure you form your own—which each of us can and should do as long as freedom survives.

- Joe Smyth, 2012

Executive Summary

76 Ways to Restore America's greatness

Citizen responsibilities

1. Free people must have the liberty to succeed or fail—so accept responsibility for yourself, your family, your neighbors, and your community.

2. Exercise your freedom, but make sure your choices don't harm others.

3. Governments don't do anything very well and get worse as they get bigger, so don't ask for a government solution to every problem.

4. Use your own common sense, but don't trust career politicians or either of the major political parties.

5. When discussing public issues, listen at least as much as you talk.

6. Be willing to learn from others, and look for win-win solutions.

7. Never engage in personal attacks, name-calling, or profanity.

8. The media wouldn't feed us so much celebrity news, political "horse race"–style coverage, and other nonsense if we didn't keep feasting on it; shallow citizens result in shallow media.

9. Don't vote if you don't have time to understand the issues.

Executive Summary

Restore the freedoms
that made America great

10. Return to the roots that made America great: lots of liberty for individuals and a minimal amount of government.

11. Stop burying citizens in hopelessly complex laws, regulations, and bureaucracies.

12. Stop economic micromanagement by the federal government.

13. Trust the long-term efficiency of free markets and the power of consumer choices.

14. Allow free markets—not government bureaucrats and politicians—to set interest rates, the value of the dollar, wages, and prices.

15. Don't allow government to become the sole provider of anything, including health care.

16. Allow patients to make their own health care choices, including legalized assisted suicide.

17. Improve educational choices, quality, innovation, and efficiency by funding students instead of bureaucracies.

18. Reaffirm that citizens with no record of felony convictions, substance abuse, or mental illness can carry firearms without the government's permission.

19. Workers must have the right to join unions, but individuals must never be forced to join a union to get a job.

20. Keep government out of religion, but be more tolerant of religious expression by individuals.

21. Keep government out of marriage, and keep religion out of civil unions.

Rein in career politicians
and special interest groups

22. Eliminate all pensions and benefits for elected officials, impose term limits and stronger conflict-of-interest rules, and cap their salaries at the median income of the private sector.

23. Ban campaign contributions by businesses, political action committees, labor unions, trade associations, and other special interest groups.

24. Cap the amount that individuals (including the candidate) can donate to a political campaign.

25. Insist on timely disclosure of all campaign contributions.

26. Require special interest lobbyists to submit their arguments in writing and post them on the Internet for public access.

27. Require members of Congress to telecommute to keep them closer to voters and get them away from the corrupting influence of Washington.

28. Limit the number of bills each lawmaker can introduce, and repeal several old laws for each new one that is adopted.

29. Require voters to have a basic knowledge of American history, the Constitution, the Bill of Rights, the branches of government, and economics.

Rein in corporate abuse and crony capitalism

30. Expose the boardroom cronyism, interlocking directorships, and fat-cat consulting firms that allow management to rip off their companies at the expense of employees and shareholders.

31. Reform corporate governance and executive compensation.

32. End government bailouts, crony capitalism, and corporate welfare.

33. Make corporate tax rates competitive globally to encourage investment.

34. Simplify corporate taxes and regulations to give small businesses a fair chance to compete.

35. Use a progressive corporate income tax to discourage monopolies and encourage the voluntary breakup of huge companies into smaller (not "too big to fail") companies.

Stop deficit spending and government waste

36. Stop burying the country—and future generations—in government debt.

37. Get government spending under control.

38. Phase out government guarantees and "insurance" (such as flood insurance).

39. Stop welfare for businesses.

40. Make government employees subject to at-will employment just like most private sector employees.

41. Simplify taxes to build trust and stop political mischief.

42. Phase in a flat tax for those with income above the poverty level.

43. Phase out tax loopholes except for charitable deductions.

44. Equalize the tax rates for income and capital gains.

45. Get control of entitlements with a broader, lower Social Security tax, gradually raise the Social Security retirement age, phase in means testing, and create win-win opt-out options for Social Security and Medicare.

46. Put the *taxpayer-funded* portion of congressional retirement accounts into the general Social Security fund.

47. Replace all federal welfare programs with a negative income tax that would give people a temporary helping hand when they most need it, remove the stigma of being on welfare, avoid class warfare, provide incentives for people to pull themselves out of poverty and climb the economic ladder, and eliminate the bureaucracy, waste, and fraud in the existing programs.

48. Cut costs associated with crime, courts, and prisons.

Limit the federal government
to its rightful roles

49. Carefully limit the role of government in order to protect individual liberty, provide more choices, and avoid political corruption.

50. Hold the federal government accountable for doing a *few* things well (the roles that are specified in the Constitution) instead of doing *everything* poorly.

51. Rein in federal government overreach and return power to state and local governments (or to the people themselves) by strictly enforcing the Tenth Amendment.

52. Stop federal funding for state and local projects.

53. Whenever the government guarantees or insures anything (such as flood insurance), it's almost always because no sane person or business will take the risk—so phase out all government guarantees.

54. Reform government compensation and rigged bidding practices to stop the rip-off of taxpayers by government unions and career politicians, and make all government contracts subject to free market competition.

55. Be suspicious of government censorship, and protect whistle-blowers.

56. Stop government incentives for unwanted babies, and allow private organizations to promote adoption and birth control.

Reform our courts,
drug policies, and prisons

57. Legalize, control, and tax drugs.

58. End the War on Drugs in order to reduce the profit motive of criminals and unburden our overloaded police, courts, and jails.

59. Legalize victimless crimes, including suicide.

60. Adopt "loser pays" rules in lawsuits.

61. Allow states to limit damages in lawsuits.

62. Use lawyer-less people's courts for minor cases.

63. Eliminate the death penalty, but require prisoners to work for their food, lodging, health care, and privileges.

Defend our national security

64. Set a good example for the rest of the world with our freedom and economic success, not with bribes and military dominance.

65. For short-term national security reasons, relax the environmental regulations that are preventing us from developing our own proven energy sources.

66. For long-term environmental reasons, tax pollution instead of regulating it.

67. Tighten border security.

68. Remove incentives for illegal immigration.

69. Be choosy about legal immigration.

70. Issue work permits (but not citizenship) to illegal immigrants who are self-supporting and have stayed out of trouble.

71. Keep a strong but tactical, defense-oriented, and efficient military.

72. Use our military technology instead of our troops.

73. Stop policing the entire world.

74. Phase out aid to foreign governments.

75. Stop funding terrorism through our dependence on foreign oil.

76. Promote liberty to the rest of the world instead of encouraging the mob rule of pure democracy.

Citizens

"It is not the function of our Government to keep the citizen from falling into error; it is the function of the citizen to keep the Government from falling into error." —Robert H. Jackson, US Supreme Court Justice

"When men yield up the privilege of thinking, the last shadow of liberty quits the horizon." —Thomas Paine, author and one of America's founders

"I do encourage you to question authority, apply logic, and think for yourself. Look at the forest, not the trees. And the centuries, not the months. Or you might risk being led willingly, as a sheep, to the slaughter." —Rick Gaber, author

What's wrong with citizens

- ***We're coasting on the sacrifices of previous generations***. America is in decline, and "we the people" haven't figured out why it's happening—much less how to restore its greatness. Our nation's founders risked everything and sacrificed tremendously to win our independence and establish a limited government devoted to the protection of individual liberty, which in turn led to America's greatness. But every generation since then has been—predictably—somewhat less passionate about those liberties and less appreciative of what we've been given, simply because it was given to us rather than earned.

- **_The political elite overwhelm us_.** Politicians and bureaucrats get paid (by us!) to do their damage full time. Citizens can't work full time at politics; we have to earn a living in the real world. This makes us more likely to fall for political rhetoric, demagoguery, knee-jerk opinions, clever slogans, and sound bites from charismatic candidates.

- **_We're drowning in red tape._** Politicians and government bureaucrats—federal, state, and local—are drowning this nation in so many rules that no citizen can possibly know all of them, much less stay in compliance. And the cost of compliance—such as needing expert help to file a tax return—takes money out of every citizen's wallet and puts an unnecessary drain on the economy.

- **_Government schools are failing_.** As labor unions and bureaucrats strengthen their control over government-run schools, students increasingly come out of those schools conditioned to depend too much on government and are unprepared to become good citizens or to earn a good living.

- ***Big Government***. Politicians (in both major political parties) get elected and reelected by being "responsive to the people," so they are happy to give us more bureaucratic complexity, wasteful spending, higher taxes, and political corruption.

- ***Vicious cycle of spending and broken promises***. When government programs don't work well (and often make problems worse), citizens make more demands and politicians make more promises. No matter how ineffective they are, government programs are almost never eliminated. Instead the politicians promise to "reform" them—usually by throwing more of OUR money at them, even if the money must be borrowed at the expense of future generations.

- ***We're too busy***. Life is complicated, and the political class keeps making it even more complicated. Most of us work hard just to earn a living and raise our families. The typical citizen simply doesn't have much time to spend on politics. This has not served us well because the average citizen has a lot more common sense than the experts to whom we have delegated our political decisions. This is a key reason for this nation steadily losing its greatness.

- **_We're all part of the problem._** Too many citizens have become dependent upon—and beholden to—big government. We want programs that benefit others to be cut, but we don't want to see any cuts to our own benefits. Special interest groups have become adept at identifying and rallying the segments of the population that are united by their government benefits and then using these groups to gain a majority in elections.

- **_A majority of "takers"?_** We are close to the time when a majority of voters can vote themselves benefits at the expense of the minority. And that's why this once-proud nation now titters on the brink of bankruptcy.

- **_A downward spiral._** The political elite will obviously not give up this game because they are the primary beneficiaries. The question is whether American citizens will wise up and insist on less government control and more individual freedom in time to restore this nation to its former greatness. The outcome is in doubt.

How to fix what's wrong with citizens

> ➤ ***Government by the people***. Citizens must learn to be suspicious of all career politicians and both of the major political parties. They are motivated by power and money, not by genuine and selfless public service. As citizens we must stop falling for the sound bites that are fed to us by the career politicians and their hired (at taxpayer expense) public relations flacks. (See the related chapters "Freedom," "Democracy," and "Political Parties.")

> ➤ ***Rein in the political elite***. We must stop honoring our political leaders and return them to their rightful place as servants of the people, not masters. Political service should always be something a citizen does for love of country and with some sacrifice—NOT for profit. Public service should always be temporary; it should never be a career. (How? See the chapters "Career Politicians," "Election Reform," and "Congressional Reform.")

> ➤ ***Limited government***. We must recognize that governments—especially big governments—don't do anything very well and often make matters even worse. Informed and intelligent citizens must insist on individual liberty and limited

government. That's precisely what they did in the glorious first 150 years of our nation's history—when America thrived at home and provided inspiration around the world. (See the related "Government" chapter.)

➤ ***Pay attention***. Citizens get the government they deserve, so we had better start paying attention. We make a huge mistake when we ask for a federal solution for every problem. Politicians are always happy to oblige by giving us even more bureaucratic complexity, more wasteful spending, higher taxes, and more political corruption. When it comes to government, smaller is better and less is more! If citizens are too lazy to pay attention, America's decline and eventual collapse are inevitable. (See the related chapters "Individual Responsibility," "Education," "Democracy," and "Freedom.")

➤ ***Don't vote if you don't understand***. "A lot of bad policies pass by popular demand," says Bryan Caplan, a professor of economics at George Mason University and author of *The Myth of the Rational Voter: Why Democracies Choose Bad Policies*. "Be honest. If you know nothing about a subject, don't have an opinion about it. And don't reward or penalize candidates for their position on an issue you don't understand."

"Don't vote; it only encourages them." —Author unknown

"It is sobering to reflect that one of the best ways to get yourself a reputation as a dangerous citizen these days is to go about repeating the very phrases which our founding fathers used in the struggle for independence." —American historian Charles A. Beard

Individual Responsibility

"People tend to forget their duties but remember their rights." —Indira Gandhi, prime minister of India

"If the American people are no damn good, then no matter how well the Constitution is written, how well we're governed, or how much good fortune comes our way, we are doomed as a nation." —Columnist John Hawkins

What's wrong with individual responsibility

- ***Individual irresponsibility.*** Too many Americans feel they are entitled: entitled to rights without responsibilities, entitled to compensation beyond what they've really earned, entitled to benefits without contributing, and entitled to free health care without taking care of their own health. (See the chapter titled "Health Care" for more about that last point.)

- ***Reckless personal spending.*** When America thrived, it was partly because earlier generations earned more than they spent and therefore had savings to invest. Politicians and Wall Street made it too easy for people to borrow against the equity in their homes so they could live far beyond their means. When the inevitable crash came, working people not only lost their homes, as taxpayers they also got stuck with the bill for government bailouts.

- ***Disregard for the rights of others***. The "me" generation doesn't seem to care about others; it's all about them. These are the people who take advantage of their customers, abuse positions of public trust for their own profit, cheat on their taxes, live beyond their means, text while driving, spend more than they should on recreational drugs or showy cars or fancy name brands, toss their cigarette butts out the car window, toss trash into the back of their pickup trucks knowing it will blow out and litter our highways, put superwide or supertall tires on their vehicles so they spray pebbles and other debris all over the cars unfortunate enough to be behind them, rig their motorcycles to make obscene amounts of noise, turn the stereo volume so high they damage the hearing of anybody nearby, put other lives at risk by disregarding speed limits, keep vicious pit bulls without proper containment, and carry on loud cell phone conversations in public places—just to name a few. (Okay, I admit it: I'm a curmudgeon!)

- **_Adult dependency_**. Children are dependent on their parents, but they are supposed to eventually grow into responsible and independent adults. Too few are making the transition. Too many of us depend on a company for our career progress, depend on schools to determine the values and education of our children, depend on doctors and drugs for our physical fitness, and depend on the government to provide for all other needs.

- **_Lazy citizenship_**. Too many voters fall for the demagoguery, false promises, class warfare, and sound bites of our politicians. Voters would rather be entertained than take the time to participate in—and help preserve—our free society.

How to fix what's wrong with individual responsibility

> ➢ ***Respect for the rights of others.*** When I was a child, my Dad taught me that "your freedom ends where the other guy's nose begins." In other words, I should be careful that my choices don't harm others. If we all lived by this simple rule, many of our laws wouldn't be necessary. (See the related "Civility" chapter.)

> ➢ ***Individual responsibility.*** A free society requires that individual citizens accept responsibility for making their own decisions and that they accept the results of their decisions without blaming others. They accept responsibility for developing a career that allows them to pay their own way and prepare for retirement. They accept responsibility for taking care of their own family and helping their neighbors. (See also the chapter titled "Freedom.")

> ➢ ***Regulatory reform.*** Government regulation of every facet of our lives increases the cost to consumers, limits consumer choice, and creates new opportunities for influence-peddling and outright fraud by politicians and bureaucrats. Reduce regulations and increase personal liberty.

➤ ***End the drug war***. It's time to recognize that real freedom must include the right to self-destruct. As explained more fully in the "Crime" chapter, legalizing drug use would reduce the profit motive of criminal drug dealers and unburden our overloaded police, courts, and jails.

➤ ***Proactive citizenship***. There's more to citizenship than voting, taxes, and jury duty. We all have an obligation to set a good example for others by being honest, truthful, responsible, hardworking, law-abiding, charitable, respectful of others, patriotic, and informed. Freedom isn't free. It's hard work. And freedom can't be kept without real effort. (Also see the "Citizens" chapter.)

"Love yourself and watch—
Today, tomorrow, always.
To straighten the crooked
You must first do a harder thing—
Straighten yourself."
—Buddha, spiritual teacher upon whose teaching Buddhism was founded

"Here are a few basic responsibilities that you, I, and all of us have as Americans: 1) It's your responsibility to pay your own way. 2) It's your responsibility to take care of your children. 3) It's your responsibility to look out for future generations of Americans. 4) You have a responsibility to be an informed voter. 5) You have a responsibility to support and defend the Constitution. 6) You have a responsibility to put America first. 7) You have a responsibility to be a good person. Honesty, honor, godliness, industry, respect for the law, morality, and truthfulness are the wheels on which our entire republic rides..." —Columnist John Hawkins

Education

"Too many of the people coming out of even our most prestigious academic institutions graduate with neither the skills to be economically productive nor the intellectual development to make them discerning citizens and voters."
—American economist and columnist Thomas Sowell

"Many public-school children seem to know only two dates: 1492 and 4th of July; and as a rule they don't know what happened on either occasion." —American writer and humorist Mark Twain

What's wrong with education in America

- ***Too many citizens aren't learning the basics***. Democracy demands that the overall population be well enough educated to make intelligent choices. If people lack critical thinking skills and the basics of economics and history, they can be misled into making political decisions that put their very freedom at risk. They'll also have difficulty supporting themselves. Our public education system is failing us.

- ***Poor outcomes***. In almost no part of American society do we spend as much money for such dismal results as we do in public education. This is mainly because the system is controlled by government bureaucrats and labor unions, competition is minimal, and many consumers (especially the poor) don't have choices.

- ***Government as the sole provider***. When we structured public education, we established government as the primary provider. As with any bureaucracy, the bigger it has gotten, the more bureaucratic it has become. When a bureaucracy starts to fail, its first instincts are to solve the problem by adding even more bureaucracy. That's what has happened to our public education system over the past few decades. The more problems we find, the more levels of costly bureaucracy we add. And the more bureaucracy we add, the more problems we create.

- ***Political meddling.*** Education is as fundamental as a teacher and students. Yet every politician in the country has a finger in the classroom. The president, Congress, and various federal agencies. The governor, state legislators, the state board of education, district school boards, state and district superintendents, and administrators. School principals, department heads, advisory councils, the PTA, teachers' unions, and individual parents. With all those layers of bureaucracy, it isn't surprising that so few of our education dollars ever find their way into the classroom. In fact, it's amazing that any learning takes place.

- ***One size doesn't fit all***. No one educational approach is right for every child. Children are different, and they learn differently; slow students get left behind or passed without acquiring basic skills and fast learners get frustrated and bored. We need a variety of educational approaches if we want to help each child achieve his or her full potential. But our government-provided education system provides us with schools that are essentially the same, with very little real diversity. Outmoded teaching methods too often bore students. Long summer vacations cause them to forget too much of what they have learned. This is especially hurtful for poorer students who may not get enough positive stimulation at home.

- ***Repressive bureaucracy***. Big government bureaucracies deny choices, limit competition, stifle creativity, ensure mediocrity, and overwhelm schools with counterproductive regulations that often have little or nothing to do with education. Public education is underperforming because it is provided by an inefficient virtual government monopoly. Our schools are run like the Soviet economy and are showing the same symptoms of failure.

- **_Self-serving unions_**. Powerful labor unions protect bad teachers at the expense of good ones, as well as stifling excellence and innovation.

- **_Frustrated teachers_**. We have plenty of talented and dedicated educators, but they are being pulled down by the system. Education naturally attracts people who want to leave the world better than they found it. While they would like to be paid decently, money isn't the most important thing in the world to them—otherwise they would have chosen another occupation. But many of the best teachers leave the system because they become frustrated with poor results, oppressive unions, unresponsive bureaucrats, and repressive red tape.

- **_Outmoded and misguided priorities_**. The structure of today's public education was designed a century ago. Today's society is more complex. The world has changed, but public education fundamentally has not. Public schools continue to invest too much in outmoded school buildings when the rest of the society has increased productivity and reduced costs by embracing the Internet and developing new technologies.

How to fix what's wrong with education in America

> ➤ ***Fund students instead of bureaucracies***. If we truly value education and want better results, we will provide funding to students instead of bureaucrats, empower schools, get government bureaucrats out of the way, and let consumers make their own choices in a free market. This country's greatness was a result of allowing individuals to make individual choices. Why not try it in education?

> ➤ ***Parental choice.*** Increasing competition and providing more choices would be the most powerful and effective education reform. Instead of funding bureaucratic and union-dominated government-run schools, allow parents to choose the best education for their children and have funding go to the child's chosen school without regard to district boundaries. Some of these schools could be run by government entities, some by entrepreneurs, some by teams of like-minded teachers, and some by not-for-profit corporations. Some could be traditional; others could be Internet based. But in order to attract and keep students, they would all have to be *good.*

➤ **_Student commitment_**. Imagine students attending schools tailored to their needs—schools that *they* had a voice in choosing. Under the present system, students are seldom asked to *commit* to a school. They are simply assigned to it. In a choice system, a student would play at least some role in the family's decision-making process. He or she might be more willing to abide by the school's rules in order to stay there. Imagine what might happen if we can get more students actually *committed* to their schools!

➤ **_Get regulators out of the classroom._** Public education can be improved only if we shift power and resources away from the central bureaucrats. Parental choice would be the ultimate regulation. If a school doesn't do a good job, parents will move their children (and their money) to a different school. This will get the politicians and regulators off the backs of the schools and break up massive school bureaucracies. Government regulations would be replaced by a student-driven system. And the thousands of school administrators who would no longer be needed could compete for teaching jobs.

➤ **_Decentralize decision making_**. Empower education providers to determine their own objectives,

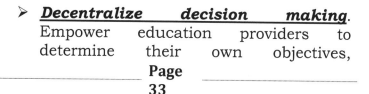

strategies, and tactics, and let them compete for students (and the funding that would come with each one). Each school could develop its own budget, curriculum, admission and discipline standards, scheduling, staffing, facilities, and investment in technology. (Especially in today's real estate environment, some schools might choose to rent or barter vacant space to free up more money for teachers and technology.)

> **_Encourage innovation and experimentation_**. With today's technologies, education could be custom-designed for each and every individual student. Individual schools (private, public, or charter) would be free to innovate, excel, and specialize in order to attract students and the funding that will come with them. Some could choose to excite their students by using educational games and new technologies. More computer-based learning could reduce the need for traditional school buildings, cut transportation costs, and give more students the opportunity to learn from the very best and most inspirational teachers.

> **_Beyond high school_**. All of the principles and solutions outlined here would apply equally to our bloated,

expensive, and underperforming public colleges and universities. Funding the students instead of the institutions would magically improve every public college and university. And since college isn't right for everybody, students should have many more choices, including trade schools.

"Twenty years from now we will look back at education as it is practiced in most schools today and wonder that we could have tolerated anything so primitive. —American educator John W. Gardner

"True education makes for inequality; the inequality of individuality, the inequality of success, the glorious inequality of talent, of genius; for inequality, not mediocrity, individual superiority, not standardization, is the measure of the progress of the world." —American educator Felix E. Schelling

"Why is it that millions of children who are pushouts or dropouts amount to business as usual in the public schools, while one family educating a child at home becomes a major threat to universal public education and the survival of democracy?" —Author Stephen Arons in *Compelling Belief: The Culture of American Schooling*

Civility

"Civilization will not last, freedom will not survive, peace will not be kept, unless a very large majority of mankind unite together to defend them and show themselves possessed of a constabulary power before which barbaric and atavistic forces will." —British statesman Winston Churchill

As citizens we have to be more thoughtful and more educated and more informed. I turn on the TV and I see these grown people screaming at each other, and I think, well, if we don't get our civility back, we're in trouble.—American singer-songwriter Emmylou Harris

What's wrong with civility in America

- ***Ugly public discourse***. The sad truth is that most American political discourse has never been very civil. Right from the beginning, people have used name-calling and distortion against those with whom they disagreed. But that doesn't make it right.

- ***Driving away decent people.*** Many uncivil extremists are so vile and hateful that they drive decent people into silence. This is the dark side of our freedom of speech.

How to restore American civility

> *__Individual restraint__.* We can and should do better, and we can do this unilaterally—one citizen at a time. No harm will come of it if we elevate the quality of our public discussions. All that is required is a bit of humility (*"I might be wrong"*), a respect for the opinions of others (*"You have as much right to your opinion as I have to mine"*), and a commitment to continuous learning (*"I can learn from others if I actually listen and think"*).

> *__No personal attacks__.* You can vigorously disagree with somebody else's opinion without attacking the individual personally. It's a matter of sticking to the issue at hand. You'll know you've gone too far when you engage in name-calling or profanity.

> *__Practice the "third alternative."__* Author Stephen Covey's *The 3rd Alternative* offers a brilliantly simple idea: If your idea is the first alternative and my idea is the second alternative, we can argue all day. But if we actually listen to one another and work at it, the third alternative we develop *together* may be far superior to your idea and mine.

> ## *Be willing to walk away.* You can quietly disengage from people who distort facts or resort to name-calling or profanity. Why waste your time with anyone who is unwilling to discuss issues in a respectful and thoughtful manner?

> ## *Not a role for government.* In a free country, civility must remain an individual choice. Citizens can reason with one another. They can choose to reject the opinions of fellow citizens who are uncivil. But the government should not get involved in defining civility or enforcing it.

"Civility costs nothing, and buys everything." —English aristocrat and writer Mary Wortley Montagu

"Aspire to decency. Practice civility toward one another. Admire and emulate ethical behavior wherever you find it. Apply a rigid standard of morality to your lives; and if, periodically, you fail—as you surely will—adjust your lives, not the standards." —English-born American broadcast journalist Ted Koppel

Career Politicians

"The American Republic will endure, until politicians realize they can bribe the people with their own money." —Alexis de Tocqueville, author of *Democracy in America*

"What this country needs are more unemployed politicians." —author Edward Langley

What's wrong with career politicians

- *__The fading American dream__*. The political elite—the so-called experts—are spoiling the American Dream. We now have a government of, by, and for the special interest groups. Members of Congress have learned that they can buy the financial support of special interest groups by voting for inappropriate federal spending. Misguided or lazy citizens are allowing them to do it; some of them actually don't seem to realize that 100 percent of "federal funds" come from taxpayers.

- *__The corruption of public office__*. It's a real ego trip to be elected to public office. The power and trappings of office soon make public officials believe they are actually better than the people they supposedly serve—and that the normal rules of decency don't apply to them.

Everybody seeks their favor, tells them how great they are, offers them money, and even refers to them with words like "honorable" and "esteemed." They hire staffers (at taxpayer expense) to stoke their egos, spread their fame, and assure their reelection. They have power, and power corrupts. Power attracts sex, money, media, fame, and eventually a feeling of invincibility. No wonder so many of them start with good intentions but end up involved in scandals.

- ***Self service, not public service***. Most first-time politicians get involved because they want to do something good for society. It doesn't take them long to realize they have to twist the truth, cut deals, and serve special interests to perpetuate their time in office. By the time they've won a couple of elections, their original good intentions are long forgotten. And the longer they remain in public office, the more arrogant and corrupt they are likely to become.

- ***Politics as a career***. When America thrived, respected citizens were recruited by their neighbors to represent them as elected public servants. These citizens served in public office reluctantly—often at great personal sacrifice—and were anxious to return to their families and occupations as soon as possible.

- ***The ruling elite***. America is in decline partly because too many of today's politicians are no longer public servants. They are instead part of a ruling elite. They are career politicians. They make little or no personal sacrifice. Most of them leave public office much wealthier than they were when they came in. Many of them have never had any other occupation, and it is doubtful they could do as well financially in any other career. Never having had a real occupation, they aren't equipped to truly represent their constituents. It's little wonder that they think government is the answer to every problem—they don't know anything except government!

- ***Too much faith in government***. Because they win elections by promising more services, politicians eventually get government involved in every facet of life—despite the proven fact that governments don't do anything very well or efficiently.

- ***Deficit spending***. Every successful business and family knows you can't spend more than you earn. Governments can't either. The trouble is that their accounting tricks, monetary manipulation, and borrowing against future generations work short-term for the career politicians who keep getting reelected—even while their actions keep contributing to the decline of America.

- ***Politics for profit***. Politicians give lots of lip service to "public service," but they have feathered their own nests at the expense of the public. Their compensation, pensions, and fringe benefits are far more generous (at taxpayer expense) than those of the people they are supposed to represent. Starting annual pay for a member of Congress is $174,000. They're usually in session fewer than 125 days a year, and after as few as five years of service they can draw a pension for the rest of their lives.

- ***Revolving golden doors***. Hundreds of former members of Congress have become lobbyists or government officials; thousands of congressional staffers have done the same. They are often promised these jobs in return for the favors they do for special interest groups while in office. This is just one more example of the corruption of career politicians.

- ***Political gridlock***. Too many politicians—often at the urging of special interest groups—paint themselves into policy corners from which no compromise is possible. "No tax increases," "no military cuts," and "no changes in Social Security" are three good examples.

- **_No real home_**. Most of the individuals elected to Congress maintain only token residences in their home district for the purpose of reelection; they're on a perpetual ego and power trip in the nation's capital, constantly fawned over and catered to by their staffers and lobbyists.

- **_Unfit for public office_**. Anybody who does what's necessary to be elected president of the United States or to Congress is unfit for the office. To a slightly smaller degree, this often holds true for the holders of lessor offices too.

How to fix America's problems with career politician

> *__Election reform__*. Special interest groups should not be permitted to make campaign contributions, and the sources and amounts of all contributions should be disclosed prior to elections. For more details, see the "Election Reform" chapter.

> *__Limit their power__*. With strict limits on the role of government, politicians will have less power. There will be fewer favors that can be granted to their cronies or denied to the enemies of their cronies. See the "Government" chapter for more about the importance of limiting the role of government.

> *__Cap their compensation__*. The salaries of elected officials should be capped at the median income of the private sector. There is no reason for politicians to earn more than the people who elect them, and it doesn't make sense for elected officials to be able to set their own pay and benefits at the expense of taxpayers. See the "Congressional Reform" chapter for proposed constitutional amendments to address congressional term limits, compensation, pensions, conflict of interest, and transparency.

> ## _**No pensions for politicians**_.
> Eliminating all pensions and fringe benefits for elected officials would help get rid of career politicians. True patriots will be willing to serve temporarily (a term or two) after having proven themselves in a real occupation, and nobody will be tempted to make a career of elected office. Politicians can participate in private health insurance, Social Security, and individual retirement accounts just like everybody else.

> ## _**Take back our money.**_ The _taxpayer-funded_ portion of congressional retirement accounts should be put into the general Social Security fund. Members of Congress should retire on Social Security and _their own_ investments like everybody else—and they certainly don't deserve to be rewarded by taxpayers for having pumped up their own pensions at our expense.

> ## _**Make them "telecommute."**_ In the Age of the Internet, there is no reason for the public's business to be done in the back rooms of Congress or the swanky bars and restaurants where lobbyists entertain members of Congress and their staffers. For more details about this proposal, see the chapter titled "Congressional Reform."

> ➤ ***Stop pumping up their egos***. Let's stop the phony tradition of automatically calling elected officials "esteemed" and "honorable." Let their performance tell us whether or not they are honorable. Former Supreme Court Justice William O. Douglas put it like this: "Since when have we Americans been expected to bow submissively to authority and speak with awe and reverence to those who represent us?"

"We hang the petty thieves and appoint the great ones to public office." —Greek writer Aesop

"Politicians need human misery. Government is a disease masquerading as its own cure." —author and political activist L. Neil Smith

"Politicians are the same all over. They promise to build a bridge even where there is no river." —Cold War Communist leader of the Soviet Union Nikita Khrushchev

Big Business

"Monopoly favors the rich (on the whole) just as competition (on the whole) favors the poor." —Author George Watson, *Journal of Economic Affairs*

"Capitalism is so successful partly because of an internal discipline that allows for loss and even bankruptcy. It's the possibility of failure that creates the opportunity for triumph. Yet many of America's major banks are too big to fail, so they can privatize profits while socializing risk...It's time to take the crony out of capitalism..." —American author and columnist Nicholas D. Kristof

What's wrong with Big Business

- ***Big Business buys politicians.*** They spend huge amounts of money on campaign contributions, lobbying, and public relations. They also dish out favors that aren't available to regular citizens, such as opportunities to participate in lucrative Wall Street initial public offerings. The politicians they support reward them with tax breaks, bailouts, favoritism in regulations, and unfair advantages over their smaller competitors. As special interests go, Big Business is every bit as bad as Big Labor, and business intrusion into government is every bit as worrisome as government intrusion into business.

- ***Government bailouts reward reckless executives.*** Big businesses keep getting bigger, often because of special treatment from the politicians they support. When reckless behavior gets the businesses in trouble, the politicians declare them "too big to fail" and use taxpayer money and credit to bail out the culprits. Then the executives reward one another with big bonuses. Nothing could be more disgraceful, and both major political parties are guilty of this practice.

- ***Obscene corporate compensation.*** There's nothing wrong with rewarding executives for building real value for their shareholders. However, big companies often engage in a form of corporate cronyism that allows top executives to feather their own nests to a much greater extent than is justified by their contributions to the company's success—and often at the expense of employees and shareholders. Interlocking directors and fat-cat consultants are a part of this game. Too many corporate boards have cozy "you scratch my back and I'll scratch yours" interlocking directorships and consulting firms. These groups are paid handsomely to justify the ridiculous compensation packages of the executives. Their excesses tend to feed class warfare, provide ammunition to socialist "reformers," and strengthen the case for government to take action.

- **_Big Business has corrupted some charities too_**. Because many top executives also sit on the boards of charities, many charities have been corrupted by the Big Business mentality. The CEOs of charities often draw exorbitant salaries—at least far more than should be necessary if the organization's goals are truly charitable. Important note: there are still many wonderful charities that have NOT been corrupted by Big Business; you can check the CEO's salary to determine which ones still deserve your support.

- **_Big Business uses government to hurt smaller competitors_**. Big businesses are run by bureaucrats, so they think like government bureaucrats. They love rules, regulations, and complexity. They can afford lots of accountants, lawyers, administrators, tax experts, and lobbyists. But the more complex things become, the harder it is for smaller businesses to compete. Big Business knows this, so they play these games brilliantly—sometimes posing as responsible reformers by supporting more regulation, fully knowing that their lobbyists can write the regulations in ways that will give them yet another advantage over their smaller competitors.

- ***Big Business is monopolistic.*** Instead of thriving on competition, many big businesses attempt to buy it out or stomp it out—often by exerting their influence on politicians and governments. They want consumers to have fewer choices because companies with near-monopoly status can charge whatever they want for their goods and services. They use their sheer size and political influence to kill off smaller competitors. Big businesses can afford, for example, to temporarily undercut prices to drive smaller competitors out of business; it's a small investment because they can jack up prices later. And they can use their profits from one near-monopoly situation to create additional near-monopoly situations. Big businesses sometimes try to bait smaller competitors into lawsuits. There they can drag the smaller company through endless legal maneuvers. Eventually the smaller company has to give up or be bankrupted by the legal fees.

- ***Big Business + Government = Trouble.*** When government meddling and Wall Street greed caused the housing boom and bust, politicians bailed out Wall Street. Corporate executives still got their obscene bonuses, and the politicians still got their obscene pensions. Working people lost their homes, and taxpayers got stuck with the government bailouts. (See the chapters "Economics" and "Government" for more about this issue.)

- ***Antitrust laws seldom work***. Government bureaucracies seldom do anything well, including enforcing antitrust laws. It's often impossible to prove anticompetitive tactics, legal fees make it too expensive for small companies to challenge bigger ones, and it's too easy for big businesses to unduly influence regulators and buy off elected officials. When government regulators do challenge a company, it's too often because that company doesn't happen to be one that's favored by the politicians in power.

How to fix the problems with Big Business

> ➤ ***Stop government bailouts***. No more government bailouts (at the expense of taxpayers) for businesses. Why should greed and bad behavior be rewarded? (But can you blame the executives when they can take big risks, reap big rewards, and pass any losses on to the taxpayers—all courtesy of our bought-and-paid-for politicians?)

> ➤ ***Corporate tax reform***. Get rid of the overly complex tax code that puts smaller businesses at a huge disadvantage in competing with larger businesses because they can't afford the accountants and tax consultants required to stay in compliance. (See "Taxes" for more about this proposal.)

> ➤ ***Progressive corporate income taxes***. A graduated corporate income tax rate would discourage monopolies and encourage the voluntary breaking up of huge companies into smaller ones. The rate could be 0 percent for smaller companies and steadily increase as companies get bigger. (More about this in the "Taxes" chapter.)

> ➤ ***Stop welfare for businesses***. Get rid of crony capitalism and let all companies

compete on a level playing field with a simplified and fairer tax code. Phase out tax loopholes and government payments to businesses, including special tax breaks to selected groups, such as oil companies and hedge fund managers. Eliminate agricultural subsidies, Amtrak subsidies, "green" incentives, government loan guarantees, and corporate bailouts. Special breaks simply open the door for more lobbying by big companies and more payoffs to politicians.

➤ **_Regulatory reform_**. Reduce the overcomplicated governmental rules, regulations, reporting requirements, and paperwork that make it so difficult for smaller companies to compete. (Big businesses can afford lobbyists to shape the government regulations and the big bureaucracies necessary to comply with the regulations; small businesses can't.)

➤ **_Election reform_**. Campaign contributions by businesses should not be permitted, and it should be a felony for a company to pressure its employees into making political contributions. (See the "Election Reform" chapter for more details about this proposal.)

➤ **_Court reform_**. Big companies sometimes use the complexity of our laws and courts to bankrupt smaller competitors with lawsuits and endless legal maneuvers. "People's courts" (in which disputes can be heard and resolved without lawyers) could go a long way toward protecting the "little guy." (Also see the "Crime, Courts, and Prisons" chapter.)

➤ ***Legislative reform.*** Businesses are being overwhelmed by the thousands of new laws that are passed each year. Limiting the number of bills that each lawmaker can introduce would force politicians to be more selective and would simplify compliance for everybody. (For more details see the "Congressional Reform" chapter.)

➤ ***Corporate governance reform.*** Executives should be rewarded for creating long-term value (new and improved products that win acceptance in the marketplace), not for short-term cost-cutting that may destroy long-term value. Stockholders should demand an end to boardroom cronyism, interlocking directorships and fat-cat consulting firms that allow management to rip off their companies at the expense of employees and shareholders. The government should not—and politicians could not be trusted to—play a role in corporate governance reform.

"The incestuous relationship between government and big business thrives in the dark." —Columnist Jack Anderson

"Politicians who talk about failed policies are just blowing smoke. Government policies succeed in doing exactly what they are supposed to do: channeling resources bilked from the general public to politically organized and influential interests groups." —Robert Higgs, author of "The Myth of 'Failed' Policies"

Big Labor

"Government touches everything in America and harms almost everything it touches. Federal, state, and local governments together spend 42 out of every 100 dollars we earn. Those who do the taxing and spending have long since ceased to work for the people as a whole. Rather, they work for themselves and for their clients —the education industry, the welfare culture, public-employee unions, etc." —Malcolm Wallop, former U.S. Senator

What's wrong with Big Labor

- ***Just another special interest***. The American labor movement served a useful purpose during the nation's manufacturing era, but it has evolved into an incredibly powerful special interest political force representing causes that often aren't in the public interest. The unions provide financial support to union-friendly politicians and expect the same kinds of political favors that Big Business expects from the politicians it supports.

- ***Government unions***. Today's most powerful unions are those that represent government employees. Union-supported politicians reward the union government employees with compensation, benefits, and work rules far more generous than needed in a free market economy. This results in taxpayers paying more than is necessary and getting less than is deserved from government.

- ***Election influence***. Politicians have learned that caving in to government union demands helps keep them in office. Government employees already make up 16 percent of voters, and they can influence family and friends to vote with them. Not surprisingly, this 32+ percent (government employees plus their families and friends) is often enough to swing the outcome of an election.

- ***Taxpayers are the victims***. One great example of the unholy partnership between Big Labor and Big Government is the requirement that nonunion companies seeking government contracts must (in effect) pay union wages and often follow union rules. This essentially shuts out the more flexible and more efficient smaller businesses—and taxpayers therefore pay more than is necessary for almost everything government does.

- ***Some union leaders rip off the members***. Just as corporate executives often rip off their companies at the expense of employees and stockholders, many union bosses get caught up in power, ego, and their own salaries at the expense of their union members. Too many unions seem to exist primarily to enrich the leaders—often at the expense of their own members as well as the rest of society.

- ***Unions are anticompetitive***. Unions don't create jobs. In fact, they limit job growth to protect the interests of their dues-paying members by insisting on wages, benefits, and work rules that exceed what would otherwise be competitive in a free market economy.

How to fix the problems with Big Labor

> ➤ ***Taxpayer pressure***. Taxpayers must wise up to the unholy alliance between government unions and politicians. They should demand that compensation of government employees be competitive with the private sector.

> ➤ ***Election reform***. Campaign contributions by labor unions should not be permitted, and it should be a felony for a union to pressure its members into making political contributions. See the "Election Reform" chapter for more details about this proposal.

> ➤ ***Right to work***. Workers must have the right to join unions, but individuals must never be forced to join a union in order to get employment. (Also see the "Freedom" chapter.)

> ➤ ***Government contract reform***. Government bids should be subject to free market competition, without union-supported politicians saddling taxpayers with the higher cost of government-mandated union wages for nonunion bidders.

"Labor unions would have us believe that they transfer income from rich capitalists to poor workers. In fact, they mostly transfer income from the large number of non-union workers to a small number of relatively well-off union workers." —Author Robert E. Anderson, *Just Get Out of the Way*

Big Media

"All of journalism is a shrinking art. So much of it is hype. The O.J. Simpson story is a landmark in the decline of journalism." —American sportswriter and broadcaster Dick Schaap

"If liberty means anything at all, it means the right to tell people what they do not want to hear." —George Orwell, English novelist and journalist

"I want the news delivered unbiased. I thought that was the whole point with journalism." —Aaron McGruder, American artist

What's wrong with Big Media

- ***Too few voices***. As big corporations have gained control of an increasing number of media outlets and driven smaller competitors under, there are fewer independent media sources.

- ***Too much infotainment.*** Americans are addicted to entertainment. Media outlets are addicted to reach and ratings. It's natural, then, that media outlets have become more concerned with entertaining people than informing and that the line between journalists and entertainers have been blurred. Straight news takes a backseat to entertainment as journalists turn themselves into clowns to attract a following.

- **_Too much opinion._** Most journalists tend to be liberal and too often allow their opinions to leak into news stories—especially in the broadcast media. Competition opens the door for diversity among stations (such Fox vs. MSNBC), but what good is diversity when each outlet is engaged in propaganda supporting a particular point of view?

- **_Horse race coverage._** More than a year prior to an election, journalists breathlessly report the latest opinion polls about candidates. This is ridiculous because opinion polls usually capture the latest knee-jerk reaction of voters who aren't very interested in an election that far in the future. Opinions tend to change dramatically once voters finally get interested enough to start thinking about the issues. But by then some candidates have been forced out of the race because of the media's fixation with premature horse race coverage.

- **_Where's the meat?_** Journalists pay so much attention to opinion polls and news-making "events" manufactured by public relations flacks that there isn't much time, space, or airtime for meaningful reporting. There is far too little original reporting about serious issues. Many journalists spend too much time chasing "the breaking story of the day" no matter how trite or meaningless it may be.

- ***Lazy citizenship***. Too many voters would rather be entertained by others than put their own time and effort into meaningful participation in a free society—so Big Media gives them what they want: entertainment.

How to fix the problems with Big Media

> ➤ ***Progressive corporate income taxes***. A graduated corporate income tax would encourage the voluntary breakup of huge media companies into smaller companies. For more details about this proposal, see the chapter titled "Taxes."

> ➤ ***Sharper citizens***. The media wouldn't keep feeding us so much celebrity news, horse race coverage, and other nonsense if people didn't keep feasting on it. Shallow citizens result in shallow media.

> ➤ ***Seek out serious journalism***. Citizens who care need to recognize and appreciate meaningful journalism. We still have some excellent reporters who can be entertaining without sacrificing their journalistic principles. They are easy to recognize because they stay focused on real issues. They don't cozy up to politicians. They aren't part of "pack journalism." They don't shout down or poke fun at others, and they don't engage in personal attacks, "gotcha" or celebrity journalism, or horse race coverage. They are able to keep their personal opinions out of their stories.

> ➤ ***More grassroots journalism***. Some of our best journalism going forward may

come from individual citizens, foundations, universities, and civil groups. Journalism was never supposed to be a licensed profession. It has always been—and must always remain—open to anybody. America's earliest journalists tended to be printers (because they owned a press), but everybody is now empowered because we all have access to the Internet. Do poor journalism, and people will ignore you; do good work, and you'll find an audience.

"The lowest form of popular culture...has overrun real journalism. Today, ordinary Americans are being stuffed with garbage." —Carl Bernstein, American investigative journalist

"If we're going to live as we are in a world of supply and demand, then journalists had better find a way to create a demand for good journalism." —Bill Kovach, author and journalist

Political Parties

"All political parties die at last of swallowing their own lies."
—*English author and satirist John Arbuthnot*

"The Democrats are the party that says government will make you smarter, taller, richer, and remove the crabgrass on your lawn. The Republicans are the party that says government doesn't work and then they get elected and prove it."
—*American author and satirist P. J. O'Rourke*

What's wrong with political parties

- ***Republicans represent special interests***. In theory Republicans stand for free enterprise and limited government. In fact, the party's primaries are usually dominated by Big Business and the Religious Right.

- ***Democrats represent special interests***. In theory Democrats stand up for the little guy. In fact, the party's primaries are usually dominated by Big Labor and lawyers.

- ***What's the difference?*** In practice (after the elections) there's not a dime's worth of difference between the two major political parties. Both parties are guilty of promising too much and delivering too little, wasting tax dollars, handing out special favors to their supporters, and increasing the national debt.

- **_Career politicians_**. Both parties usually nominate career politicians who have only one real priority: their own reelection. In public, they give lip service to their voters and to the nation's well-being. Then, behind closed doors, they cut deals that take care of their real masters—the special interest groups that finance their campaigns.

How to fix what's wrong with political parties

> ➤ ***Election reform***. Only individuals should be allowed to make campaign contributions to politicians and political parties. Big Business, Big Labor and anonymous special interest political action committees (PACs) should not have the controlling influence they currently enjoy. (For more details about this proposal, see the "Election Reform" chapter.)

> ➤ ***Limited government.*** With strict limits on the role of government, political parties will have less power. (See the "Government" chapter for more about this issue.)

> ➤ ***Force Congress to telecommute***. See the "Congressional Reform" chapter for more details about this proposal.

"When politicians want to do nothing, and yet look like they are doing something, they appoint a blue ribbon committee or go to the U.N. or assign some Cabinet member to look into the problem and report back to the President —hoping that the issue will be forgotten by the time he reports back." —Thomas Sowell, American economist, author and columnist

Political Parties

"Political parties, overanxious for vote catching, become tolerant to intolerant groups." —Wendell Willkie, 1940 Republican candidate for U.S. President

Election Reform

"A government which robs Peter to pay Paul can always depend on the support of Paul." —Irish playwright George Bernard Shaw

"Politics is the gentle art of getting votes from the poor and campaign funds from the rich, by promising to protect each from the other." —Oscar Ameringer, socialist and labor organizer

What's wrong with our elections

- ***Voter gullibility***. Uninformed voters can doom any democracy. Too many voters complete their public education without a basic understanding of American history, the Constitution, the Bill of Rights, the branches of government, and economics. Many avoid politics until Election Day, and then base their votes on the superficial and often intentionally misleading sound bites or attack ads from the politicians who will stoop to almost any level to get elected.

- ***Money rules***. There's too much money in political campaigns, and most of it comes from special interests. All other things being equal, the biggest spender wins. That's usually because the biggest spender can hire the slickest campaign staffers—the ones who best know how to use demagoguery and sound bites to win elections.

- ***Special interests have the money.*** This means candidates often sell their souls to the special interest group that can provide the most money. This usually means Big Business support for Republicans and Big Labor, and trial lawyer support for Democrats.

- ***Politicians play a self-serving game.*** It doesn't take politicians long to figure out that they can win elections by promising to take care of people. So they make promises to voters, create more bureaucracies to "serve the people," construct more rules to make sure everybody performs to the government's standards, and create even more bureaucracies to enforce the rules. At some point, which in large measure is NOW, government is no longer limited, individuals are no longer free, and insolvent America is no longer an inspiration to other nations.

How to fix the problems with our elections

> ➤ ***Election reform***. Only individuals should be allowed to make campaign contributions to politicians. Campaign contributions by businesses, political action committees, labor unions, trade associations, and other special interest groups should not be permitted. (It is ridiculous to argue that these groups are entitled to free speech in the form of campaign contributions. Free speech is an *individual* liberty, and this right can only be diminished by extending it to special interest groups.)

> ➤ ***No tampering by special interest groups***. It should be a felony for special interest groups to unduly pressure their members or employees into making political contributions by threatening them, underwriting any individual's contribution, or promising anything of value.

> ➤ ***Full & early disclosure of all contributions***. No contributions should be allowed within a month of the election, and full disclosure of the amount and source of all contributions should be posted online at least two weeks prior to the election.

➢ ***Constitutional Amendment***. If citizens put enough pressure on them, members of Congress could be forced to impose bold campaign finance reforms. If Congress fails to act, a citizen-driven constitutional amendment—as described in the "Take Back Congress" chapter—may be necessary. It could be worded something like this: "Candidates for elected federal offices shall accept campaign contributions only from individual citizens. Campaign contributions by businesses, political action committees, labor unions, trade associations, and other groups shall not be permitted. All campaign contributions must be made a least one month prior to the applicable election, and full disclosure of the amount and source of each contribution shall be posted online at least two weeks prior to the election."

➢ ***Less campaign spending***. There would be less money spent if we limit campaign contributions to individuals, cap the amounts that individuals (including the candidate) can donate, require that contributions be made at least a month prior to the election, and require full and timely disclosure of contributions. Less campaign spending would be a big improvement. Fewer political ads, fewer sound bites and fewer politician robo-calls wouldn't hurt anything. Even with less money to spend, each candidate could still reach voters via a comprehensive website outlining his or her positions, as well as by issuing press releases and participating in candidate debates.

> ➤ ***Competent voters.*** Does it make any sense that we require people to qualify for a driver's license, but there are no limits except age on who can vote? States should develop competency tests for voters to determine whether they have at least a basic understanding of American history, the Constitution, the Bill of Rights, the branches of government, and economics. The federal government could properly challenge any state law that violates the Fifteenth Amendment, which prohibits denying the vote because of a person's race or color.

"No one will really understand politics until they understand that politicians are not trying to solve our problems. They are trying to solve their own problems—of which getting elected and re-elected are number one and number two. Whatever is number three is far behind."—Economist and columnist Thomas Sowell

Congressional Reform

"There is no distinctly Native American criminal class...save Congress." —American author and humorist Mark Twain

"If pro is opposite of con, then what is the opposite of progress?" —Attributed to a makeshift sign in a men's restroom, House of Representatives, Washington, DC

What's wrong with Congress

- ***A loss of confidence***. Citizens have lost confidence in Congress, and it's no wonder! Members of Congress stay too long, spend too much time raising funds for reelection, are too influenced by special interest lobbyists, and are too far removed from the people they are supposed to represent.

- ***The best people don't stay***. Congress is too tradition-bound, seniority-dominated, inefficient, money-driven, and ineffective. Indeed, that's why some of the finest people never run for Congress or else walk away from it in frustration instead of making it a career. The ones who stay usually end up far wealthier than they were when they got elected.

- ***It's too corrupt and too expensive***.
  Members of Congress move to
  Washington to party with lobbyists, hire
  staffers (at taxpayer expense) whose
  primary mission is to ensure that their
  boss gets reelected, and stick taxpayers
  with travel costs for frequent trips back
  to their district to ensure they stay in
  office.

How to fix what's wrong with Congress

> ➢ ***Fewer laws***. Individuals and businesses are being overwhelmed by the thousands of new laws that are passed each year. Citizens should urge that our politicians repeal three to five laws for every new one that is passed. Limiting the number of bills that each lawmaker can introduce would force them to be more selective and would simplify compliance for everybody. In addition, every new law should be written in plain English instead of language only a lawyer can understand. If we took these approaches, citizens would have a better chance of actually understanding society's rules.

> ➢ ***Bold, radical reform***. Bold reforms that bring real progress usually occur only in times of crisis. The United States is clearly in crisis now with budget deficits resulting from years of weak leadership, political gridlock, and outright corruption in Washington. Why not begin the reform precisely where most of the problems originate—with Congress itself?

> ➢ ***Rein in the career politicians***. A nation that wants to remain free will choose its leaders from among successful citizens who serve temporarily

and then return to productive society. Capping the pay of public officials, eliminating their special benefits and pensions, and imposing term limits would be a good start.

> ***Limit their power.*** With strict limits on the role of government, Congress will have less power. There will be fewer favors that can be granted to supporters or denied to opponents. See the "Government" chapter for more discussion about the importance of limiting the role of government.

> ***Stronger conflict of interest rules***. It's ridiculous that members of Congress can benefit from perks such as post-Congress jobs, insider trading profits, and access to initial public offerings that aren't available to regular citizens. Former members of Congress should be banned from any government or special interest employment for at least four years after serving in Congress.

> ***What if Congress won't reform itself?*** If citizens put enough pressure on them, politicians could be forced to adopt meaningful reforms. If they fail to do so, constitutional amendments may be necessary, as described in the "Take Congress Back" chapter. The first new amendment could be worded something like this: No individual may serve more than twelve years in the United States Congress.

Congressional salaries may not exceed the median income of citizens. There shall be no pensions or benefits for elected federal officials beyond Social Security and their own self-funded retirement accounts and insurance policies. Elected federal officials shall not accept any gift with a value exceeding $100, participate in initial public stock offerings or insider trading, or accept any government or government influence–related employment for at least four years after leaving office.

➤ ***Rein in lobbyists & increase transparency***. Again, enough pressure from citizens could force Congress to impose bold reforms. If not, another citizen-driven constitutional amendment may be necessary. This one could be worded something like this: "Any citizen or group that wishes to influence congressional legislation must submit their positions in writing. Any verbal communications with members of Congress about pending legislation must be followed by a confirming memo. With the exception of sensitive national security issues, transcripts of all congressional hearings shall be posted on the Internet for public access. All communications to members of Congress regarding specific legislation shall be posted on the Internet for public access at least twenty-four hours prior to congressional votes. Members of Congress shall be permitted to cast their votes electronically, so their physical presence in the nation's capital will no longer be necessary."

➤ ***Make them telecommute***. Keep members of Congress out of Washington (where they're too tempted by lobbyists and too full of their own self-importance) and send them home (where they'll stay closer to taxpayers and do less harm). With today's technologies, members of Congress could use their computers, iPads, or iPhones to study issues, consider lobbyist arguments, participate in hearings and debates, and cast their votes—all on the Internet and visible to the public. (A two-week annual retreat could allow legislators enough time to meet newly-elected members and develop working relationships with one another.)

> ***A telecommuting Congress***. Salaries are just the tip of the iceberg when it comes to legislative expenses. A telecommuting Congress would save taxpayers tens of millions of dollars annually in travel expenses, office space, mailings, telephones and faxes, secretarial support, and printing costs. Even more important...

> ***Open up the process***. With a telecommuting Congress, congressional service would no longer be a full-time or elitist job. Because our lawmakers would work from their homes, any citizen could serve—even those with real jobs and family responsibilities. The entire process would be open to all citizens. People who might never be able to attend a legislative hearing could read position

papers and post their comments online at virtual public hearings.

➤ ***Quality would improve***. A telecommuting Congress would eliminate a great deal of political cronyism and replace it with merit-based analysis and discussion of issues. Lobbyists would have to make their cases in online position papers that would be posted for all to see instead of peddling their influence privately in back rooms, bars, and restaurants. Instead of meeting with special interest lobbyists, congressional staffers could spend more time studying issues, and their analyses could be posted online along with the submissions from citizens, cabinet members, and lobbyists.

➤ ***Stop the pomp and circumstance***. In a free society, there should be no office higher than citizen. There is no reason to call anybody "The Honorable" just because the person has been elected to office. The performance of our elected officials will tell us whether or not they are honorable.

➤ ***Ditto for state and local governance***. Variations of many of the recommendations in this chapter could be applied to state and local governments, too.

"In my many years I have come to a conclusion that one useless man is a shame, two is a law firm and three or more is a congress." —John Adams, American founder, lawyer and political theorist

"No man's life, liberty, or property is safe while the legislature is in session." —American author and humorist Mark Twain

"Talk is cheap...except when Congress does it." —Unknown

Censorship

"Censorship reflects a society's lack of confidence in itself."
—U.S. Supreme Court Justice Potter Stewart

"A government by secrecy benefits no one. It injures the people it seeks to serve; it damages its own integrity and operation. It breeds distrust, dampens the fervor of its citizens and mocks their loyalty." —U.S. Senator Russell B. Long

What's wrong with censorship

- ***All-powerful government***. People who entrust the government with the power of censorship give up the only means they have to ensure a "government of, for, and by the people." Dictatorships often emerge when the government holds the power to censor.

- ***Political or military secrets?*** Too many Americans are willing to accept political censorship, often confusing the issue with the legitimate need for some secrets during wartime. It's important to distinguish between the two.

How to fix the problems with censorship

> ➤ ***Safeguard freedom of speech and press***. Political censorship can't be tolerated in a free society. People must have the right to voice their opinions, no matter how unpopular those opinions may be. There is little harm in letting those voices be judged in the court of public opinion and much potential harm if they cannot be heard. History proves that governments can never be trusted to decide what the people can and cannot be permitted to know.

> ➤ ***Be suspicious of any censorship***. Even in times of war, citizens should be wary of government censorship. It's far too easy for the government and its military to extend censorship far beyond what is actually necessary—often to cover their own butts, hide their mistakes, or misrepresent their real motives. Besides, a more enlightened approach to America's military involvement around the world should limit the need for war secrets. (For more details, see the chapter titled "National Security.")

> ➤ ***Protect whistle-blowers***. Whistle-blowers are essential in a free society. Citizens should be quick to protest when the government tries to prosecute

whistle-blowers because it is usually an attempt to silence government critics or hide the truth from the public. (See also the chapter titled "Citizens.")

"Censorship always defeats its own purpose, for it creates, in the end, the kind of society that is incapable of exercising real discretion...In the long run it will create a generation incapable of appreciating the difference between independence of thought and subservience." —American historian Henry Steele Commager

"Sometimes sunlight is the best disinfectant." —U.S. Supreme Court Justice Louis Brandeis

"The liberties of a people never were, nor ever will be, secure, when the transactions of their rulers may be concealed from them." — American founder and orator, Patrick Henry

Freedom

"The lesson that Americans today have forgotten or never learned—the lesson which our ancestors tried so hard to teach—is that the greatest threat to our lives, liberty, property, and security is not some foreign government, as our rulers so often tell us. The greatest threat to our freedom and well-being lies with our own government!" —American libertarian Jacob G. Hornberger

"Freedom is not empowerment. Anybody can grab a gun and be empowered. It's not entitlement. An entitlement is what people on welfare get, and how free are they? It's not an endlessly expanding list of rights—the 'right' to education, the 'right' to health care, the 'right' to food and housing. That's not freedom, that's dependency. Those aren't rights, those are rations of slavery—hay and a barn for human cattle. There's only one basic human right, the right to do as you damn well please. And with it comes the only basic human duty, the duty to take the consequences." —American author and satirist P. J. O'Rourke

"The policy of American government is to leave its citizens free, neither restraining them nor aiding them in their pursuits." —Thomas Jefferson, third US president

What's wrong with freedom in today's America

- **_Governments stifle human greatness._** Individual freedom and individual initiative have made America the most successful economy in world history, but misguided people are leading us in the wrong directions. When government makes the decisions—as it increasingly does in America—individuals are marginalized and individual initiative fades.

- **_The human spirit wants to be free._** Humans innately want to be free. Given the freedom to make our own decisions and reap the rewards of our work, the vast majority of individuals will generally make good choices, work hard, and become successful.

- **_The human spirit wants to be generous._** Most people are decent and well-meaning. We want our lives to be meaningful. We want to help those around us become happy and successful. The more successful we become, the more inclined we are to want to help those in need.

- **_Socialism doesn't work._** It may sound good to many of us (especially in our idealistic youth), but socialism has been tried numerous times and just doesn't work. As a journalist, I was able to visit and observe the Soviet Union at its peak. It was clear even then that central planners were failing in their efforts to turn people into mindless zombies. People want to be free. They want to make their own choices.

- ***Free markets work***. The only proven way to increase prosperity and reduce poverty is through individual liberty, capitalism, and free markets. Millions of people from around the world have wanted to come to America so they, too, could have the freedom to make their own decisions and be responsible for their own success.

- ***We've forgotten what made us great***. American greatness was achieved because the founders fought hard and sacrificed dearly for American independence, individual liberties, and limited government. They feared and distrusted rulers. They believed in the individual, so they created a Constitution that gave lots of freedom to individuals and sharply limited the role of government.

- ***We didn't have to earn it***. American greatness is declining now because the country has drifted steadily away from individual liberty and toward an all-powerful and all-encompassing government. It's natural that people who didn't have to fight for their freedom would start taking it for granted. And some begin to wonder why—in such a wealthy nation—they can't be taken care of instead of having to work for a living. It is important to remember that tyrants always use "the good of the people" as their reason for taking power away from the citizens.

- ***Complexity kills freedom***. "There ought to be a law!" That's a common response—often from special interest groups—whenever somebody thinks there is a problem. Politicians happily oblige by passing a law, even though we all know most laws are poorly conceived, poorly drafted, and often counterproductive. There are far too many laws and regulations, and many are far too vague and complex; businesses and citizens are being overwhelmed by the volume of legislation passed each year. When there are so many laws and regulations that citizens can't even be aware of all of them, every citizen is at risk of unintentionally being in violation of something.

- ***Overlapping layers of government***. What's worse, all four levels of government (federal, state, county, and local) often create overlapping laws dealing with the same issue. Each law, in turn, comes with bureaucrats, fees, taxes, and rules and regulations intended to enforce the law. That's why the typical citizen can't fill out a tax return or government application without professional help. It also explains why most small businesses are overwhelmed by bureaucratic requirements. No free society can continue to exist under the weight of so much regulation and bureaucracy. This is one of the reasons why America is in decline.

- ***An avalanche of laws and regulations***. Laws and regulations almost never get repealed. The politicians and bureaucrats just keep adding more. There are so many laws that the typical citizen has no hope of knowing what they are. This means that every one of us is likely guilty of violating some vague and complex law or regulation and is therefore subject to arrest or harassment by overzealous or vindictive authorities. Ignorance of the law is no defense. When there are so many laws that virtually everybody is "guilty" of *something*—no matter how obscure the law may be—*everybody* is at risk of government oppression. Those in power—whether elected officials or government bureaucrats—can favor their friends and punish their enemies with selective drafting of laws or selective enforcement. When the political elite make rules that are too complicated for the typical citizen to cope with, the seeds of tyranny are planted.

- **_Power corrupts_**. The bigger and more powerful things become, the worse they tend to get. Eventually, the people running the bureaucracy put their own interests ahead of the interests of the people they are supposed to serve. This is true of corporations, labor unions, special interest groups, and—most especially and most dangerously—governments.

- **_Rules stifle common sense_**. The bigger an organization becomes, the more bureaucratic it becomes. As bureaucracies grow bigger and more powerful (as they inevitably do), more rules are imposed. Common sense, individual choices, and good judgment disappear. People are treated like cogs in a machine rather than as unique individual human beings. The brilliance and passion of individuals is stifled by the rules of the bureaucracy.

- **_Bureaucrats cut deals to get more power_**. When powerful bureaucrats form self-serving alliances and cut deals—such as the ones between business and labor, business and government, or government and labor—everybody suffers except the bureaucrats in charge.

How to fix what's wrong with freedom in America

> **_Return to common sense_**. Americans must regain some common sense. With the nation in steady decline, it must happen now—before it's too late. We must recognize that the government can't take care of us, and that the politicians and political elite who make such promises are only doing so to enrich themselves and ensure their reelection. (See also the chapter titled "Career Politicians.")

> **_Don't ask for government solutions_**. Government solutions often make the problem worse, so let's stop saying "there ought to be a law" and instead work with other citizens and the private sector to find solutions. (See also the chapter titled "Citizens.")

> **_Limit the role of governments_**. Let's carefully define the legitimate role of each level of government so we don't have four layers of government—local, county, state, and federal—all trying to solve the same problems.

> **_Especially limit federal roles_**. The federal government's roles should be strictly limited, as discussed in more depth in the chapter titled

"Government." Most things are best left to smaller units of state or local government, or—even better—to the people themselves.

> **_Simplify the rules_**. Freedom is being overwhelmed by the thousands of new laws that are passed each year. If we limited the number of bills that each lawmaker can introduce, citizens would have a better chance of actually understanding society's rules. (See the "Congressional Reform" chapter for more details about this proposal.)

> **_Legalize suicide_**. In a free society, suicide must be a personal choice. Laws against suicide should therefore be repealed. (See more about this in the "Religion" chapter.)

> **_Get rid of career politicians_**. A nation that wants to remain free will choose its leaders from among successful citizens who would serve temporarily and then return to productive society. (How? See the "Career Politicians" and "Election Reform" chapters.)

> **_Individual choices_**. Make sure every organization to which you belong respects the individual rights of every constituent. When an organization becomes too big, too bureaucratic, too powerful, too complex, or too

unresponsive, leave and consider joining or starting a rival group.

➢ ***Keep it small and local***. As discussed more fully in the chapter titled "Government," decisions should be made at the most practical local level where bureaucracy can be kept to a minimum and people are best equipped to recognize political nonsense.

➢ ***Return to our roots***. To stop America's decline, we must return to the roots that made this nation great: a maximum amount of liberty for individuals and a minimum amount of government.

"Although we give lip service to the notion of freedom, we know that government is no longer the servant of the people but, at last, has become the people's master. We have stood by like timid sheep while the wolf killed—first the weak, then the strays, then those on the outer edges of the flock, until at last the entire flock belonged to the wolf." —Gerry Spence, lawyer and author, *From Freedom to Slavery*

"Regulation hurts the people the politicians claim to help. People once just went into business. But now, in the name of 'consumer protection,' bureaucrats insist on licensing rules. Today, hundreds of occupations require expensive licenses. Tough luck for a poor person getting started. Once upon a time, one in 20 workers needed government permission to work in their occupation. Today, it's one in three. We lose some freedom every day. This is not what America was supposed to be." —American author and journalist John Stossel

"When you see that trading is done, not by consent, but by compulsion—when you see that in order to produce, you need to obtain permission from men who produce nothing—when you see that money is flowing to those who deal, not in goods, but in favors—when you see that men get richer by graft and by pull than by work, and your laws don't protect you against them, but protect them against you—when you see corruption being rewarded and honesty becoming a self-sacrifice—you may know that your society is doomed. —Ayn Rand, author, *Atlas Shrugged*

Bigotry & Government

"I don't much care who is gay or straight or married or not. I mostly notice if they are brave enough to confront bigotry."
—American actress, singer and dancer Jasmine Guy

What's wrong with bigotry and government

- ***A people divided***. The country is too often torn apart by fierce battles over issues that shouldn't divide us at all. A nation that's built on freedom, individual liberties, property rights, and the rule of law simply must make those things available equally to all its citizens. Some people may always harbor bias toward those who are different, but the government should never participate in such biases.

- ***Human rights for all***. This nation can be proud that government no longer discriminates against people on the basis of race, creed, or national origin. (Government sometimes goes too far with quotas and reverse discrimination, but that's a separate issue.) The next frontier is to end government bias against people on the basis of gender.

- ***Gay marriage***. The nation is divided on this issue partly because both sides want to use the force of law to impose their beliefs about marriage on everybody else. In a country based on individual liberty, this is entirely unnecessary.

- ***Marriage and law are an odd and incompatible couple***. Marriage in the United States has evolved as an odd mixture of religious ceremony and legal arrangement. The two simply don't go well together, and that's what causes all the friction and disagreement.

How to fix the problems with bigotry and government

> ## *Divorce government from marriage.*
> To the government, marriage should be nothing more than a legal document between consenting adults, regardless of their gender, race, or religious beliefs. It should be a matter of equal treatment under the law. Consenting adults should be free to enter into whatever legal arrangements they wish, on whatever terms to which they and their partner agree. Freedom of religion means the government shouldn't be involved in the traditional religious aspects of marriage. Government might help clarify the issue by substituting the words "civil union" for "marriage" in all laws, government regulations, and tax codes.

> ## *Marriage is for churches.* Churches
> should remain free to recognize or not recognize various types of marriages as they see fit. If some churches don't wish to recognize gay marriage, they should have that right. Individuals would have that right as well. Couples who want a church wedding in addition to their legal agreement would be free to arrange for both.

> ## *End reverse discrimination.* Two
> wrongs don't make things right. Some

laws and regulations have resulted in reverse discrimination, such as race-based hiring quotas or admission standards. Free people don't need those kinds of favors from the government. All they need is freedom and equal treatment under the law. Freedom ends when government attempts to force equal outcomes. (See also the "Freedom chapter.")

"I believe all Americans who believe in freedom, tolerance and human rights have a responsibility to oppose bigotry and prejudice based on sexual orientation." —American author and civil rights activist Coretta Scott King

"Too small is our world to allow discrimination, bigotry and intolerance to thrive in any corner of it, let alone in the United States of America." —U.S. Congressman Elliot Engel

Health Care

"If you think health care is expensive now, wait until you see what it costs when it's free!" —American author and humorist P. J. O'Rourke

What's wrong with health care

- ***There is no "free lunch."*** There is no such thing as free medical care (or free anything else) from the government. As explained in the "Government" chapter, government can only take money from some people and give it to others—and it does an incredibly inefficient job of this because its ever-expanding bureaucracies take so much off the top.

- ***Government is the problem, not the solution***. The government's tax code favors employer-provided health insurance. This keeps millions of Americans captive to their employer's health plan, limits competition, and reduces consumer choices.

- ***Consumers are buffered from real costs***. An army of third-party bureaucracies (employers, government, and insurance companies) come between patients and doctors. In 1961 individuals directly paid 47 percent of their health care costs. Clearly, they still had an incentive to spend wisely. By 2011 individuals directly paid only 12 percent of their health care costs. When you consider these statistics, it isn't surprising that consumers have lost much of the incentive to use common sense in making their health care choices and to hold providers accountable for the costs and results. (In reality, consumers as a group ultimately pay 100 percent of the cost, plus the overhead of all the insurance companies, employer bureaucracies, and government agencies that come between consumers and health care providers.)

- ***Too many people don't accept personal responsibility***. With government, employers, and insurance companies seemingly responsible for our health, too many citizens don't take care of themselves. They continue to abuse alcohol and drugs, drive recklessly, eat the wrong kinds of food—and eat far too much of it—and avoid exercise. The attitude is that people can abuse their health and then be "fixed" by doctors, with insurance companies or the government paying the costs.

- ***Government regulations drive up medical costs.*** In attempting to do for citizens what they don't believe citizens can do for themselves, bureaucrats have burdened doctors and hospitals with endless regulations that drive up health care costs as well as the cost of medical insurance. Laws that make suicide illegal are just one example.

- ***Greedy lawyers drive up medical costs***. Medical professionals are forced to pay outrageous premiums for malpractice insurance. To protect themselves from malpractice suits, they often order unnecessary tests. Both of these practices drive up medical costs. Fast-talking, money-grubbing lawyers have taken a great American justice system and distorted it beyond recognition. It's no longer about justice but rather about how lawyers can become richer at the expense of the rest of society.

- ***Uninsured patients drive up medical costs.*** Many poor people simply can't afford medical insurance. Many more could afford it but choose not to have it because they figure society will take care of them even if they don't take care of themselves. (And society does take care of the uninsured. When they're sick enough, they show up in hospital emergency wards. The hospitals treat them and pass the unreimbursed costs along to those who do pay.)

- **_Regulations limit treatment options and drive up costs_**. Government regulations drive up costs and severely limit the choices available to medical professionals and their patients. Instead of allowing patients and doctors to make their own choices, the government decides. It drives up costs by forcing drug companies through cumbersome approval processes and limits treatment options by denying experimental drugs to dying patients.

- **_Doctor quality declining_**. Government regulations are making medical careers more difficult and less rewarding. Why should our best and brightest young people go to school for so long, come out with so much debt, and then have their medical decisions and compensation dictated by bureaucrats? Doctors are already increasingly rushing patient care and taking more shortcuts to meet government insurance standards. This will ultimately lead to fewer and less talented doctors and lower quality care.

- **_Outrageous end-of-life medical costs_**. Because of government regulations and the fear of lawsuits, families and care providers often feel compelled to provide more end-of-life medical care than the patient actually wants. The fact that insurance will cover the costs influences family decisions, greed is sometimes a factor for the care providers, and patients often have to endure a lot more suffering than should be necessary.

How to fix what's wrong with health care

> ➤ ***Get the government out of the insurance business.*** Government-run health insurance plans—including Medicare and Medicaid—should be gently phased out. If nobody except the government is willing to provide insurance, it means it's a bad deal for taxpayers too. (See more about this point in the "Government" chapter.)

> ➤ ***Negative income tax.*** The federal government should replace all its failing poverty programs with a brilliantly simple negative income tax that would allow everybody to buy insurance to at least cover catastrophic health issues. (See the "Poverty" chapter for details about how the negative income tax would work.)

> ➤ ***"Skin in the game."*** It's important for patients to have a direct financial stake in the cost of their medical care, as well as a voice in treatment options. Higher copays and higher deductibles would cause consumers to make more responsible decisions about which treatment plans are necessary and worth the investment, while insurance could still provide coverage for catastrophic health issues. Health Savings Accounts

(HSAs) could also be an important part of the solution.

> **_Less government regulation_**. Doctors and patients need to be free to make their own medical decisions. They will do precisely that if the government stops trying to micromanage everybody's health care. True, some doctors and patients will make poor choices—but isn't that what freedom is all about? And do we really want politicians and bureaucrats making decisions about *our* medical care?

> **_More competition_**. Some state insurance regulators interfere with free markets and sometimes grant semi-monopolies to insurers. Consumers would have more choices --- and insurance companies would be more innovative and efficient --- if state regulators allowed insurance companies to sell policies across state lines.

> **_More freedom and responsibility_**. With freedom comes responsibility. Each of us should do a better job of making our families—and our health care providers—aware of our medical preferences. We will be more likely to do this if we know that insurance won't entirely buffer our family from the costs. More of us might choose healthier

lifestyles, less medical treatment, less suffering, and a more dignified death.

> ***More innovation***. One of the advantages of getting government out of health care is that more innovation could take place. With the government's one-size-fits-all approach, sick people have to visit a doctor (sometimes several doctors) and make additional energy-consuming trips for tests. Too many of us end up in hospitals—which often make us even sicker. Many patients could benefit from medical care provided via some combination of telephone, e-mail, the Internet and at-home care. And with today's technologies, these alternative services might be safer, more effective, and less expensive.

> ***Legalize suicide***. In a free society, suicide should be a personal choice. Laws against suicide should be repealed. (See more about this in the "Religion" chapter.)

> ***Limit damages***. Not every wrong can be made right; sometimes life isn't fair. States can set reasonable limits on damages that can be awarded in civil cases, including malpractice suits. When an ambulance-chasing lawyer convinces jurors to make an outrageous award, the cost ultimately falls to consumers in the form of higher insurance rates.

"We need not speculate as to what effects price controls can have on medicines and medical care because there are already shortages of both in countries where a government-controlled medical system includes price controls."—Thomas Sowell, American economist and columnist

Abortion

"I am pro-choice, but I find that abortion is a failure of the feminist establishment. With every kind of birth control available in the world, abortion is not something to be proud of. If you need an abortion, you've failed." —Tammy Bruce, American radio talk show host

What's wrong about America's abortion battles

- ***A divided nation.*** Many Americans oppose "abortion on demand," but would support abortion in exceptional cases such as rape or when the health of the mother and child are at risk. Yet the abortion issue continues to tear the country apart.

- ***Pro-lifers***. Government should never condone the taking of a human life, but the efforts of pro-life activists usually result in lawmakers defining under what circumstances abortions CAN be conducted legally. Is this really what the pro-lifers want?

- ***Pro-choicers***. The pro-choice activists have it wrong too. Abortion isn't a question of women's rights. The government should never condone the taking of a human life, but that's essentially what pro-choicers often advocate with their efforts to legalize abortion entirely.

- **_Can't be policed_**. Some things are impossible to police without unacceptable government meddling in the private lives of its citizens. Abortion is a prime example. The mother has the power to unilaterally terminate a pregnancy in a wide variety of ways that the government is unable to prevent. Besides, the morning-after pill and other developments may make the "life vs. choice" debate a moot point.

- **_Black market abortions_**. Government efforts to prevent abortions inevitably result in more unwanted pregnancies being terminated in dangerous back-alley abortions. Even if government could effectively prevent abortions, desperate people would still find other ways to terminate unwanted pregnancies.

- **_Welfare babies_**. The government's current approaches to welfare encourage the wrong behaviors—such as giving birth to unwanted children in order to increase welfare amounts.

- ***<u>Single-issue politicians</u>***. By making abortion the single issue in elections, we have elected far too many politicians who are ill-prepared to deal with any issue other than abortion.

How to fix what's wrong with America's abortion battles

> ➤ ***Stop government incentives for unwanted babies***. Replacing all existing welfare programs with a negative income tax would remove the financial incentive for the poor to bring more unwanted babies into the world. See more about this point in the chapter titled "Poverty."

> ➤ ***Education***. Educate the public about the many problems caused by unwanted pregnancies—and the many methods of preventing them. (Best done by individuals and private organizations, not by the government.)

> ➤ ***Promote adoption***. For those who aren't ready to be parents, promote adoption as a moral alternative to abortion and as a wiser choice than single motherhood—and provide support to those who choose to offer their baby for adoption. (Best done by individuals and private organizations, not by the government.)

"Abortion politics have distracted all sides from what is really essential: a major aid campaign to improve midwifery, prenatal care and emergency obstetric services in poor countries." —American columnist Nicholas D. Kristof

"It is now quite lawful for a Catholic woman to avoid pregnancy by a resort to mathematics, though she is still forbidden to resort to physics or chemistry." —American journalist and satirist H. L. Mencken

Guns

"Expecting a carjacker or rapist or drug pusher to care that his possession or use of a gun is unlawful is like expecting a terrorist to care that his car bomb is taking up two parking spaces." —American author Joseph T. Chew

What's wrong with America's debate about guns

- *Extremism*. Many people on both sides of the gun control issue are overly extreme in their positions. On the one side are people who want everybody to be free to possess firearms, without any government control whatsoever, to prevent governments from creating "victim zones" composed of unarmed law-abiding citizens. On the other side are people who want to deny firearms to everybody except the government's military and police forces, as they incorrectly believe banning firearms will dramatically lower the violent crime rate.

- *Unrealistic expectations*. Government doesn't do anything very well. But even if the government could do a good job with gun control, murderers will always find a way to commit murder just as thieves will always find a way to steal. Once guns are banned, will government ban razor blades, bricks, stones, and kitchen knives?

- ***Tragic outcomes***. We don't seem to be able to keep guns out of the hands of fanatics and the mentally ill. When sane people are unarmed, mass murders can be carried out in schools, shopping malls, and even military bases because there's nobody in the crowd who can stop the murderer. And when it is *seconds* that count, the police are *minutes* away.

How to fix what's wrong with America's gun policies

> ➤ ***Reaffirm our right to bear arms.*** Citizens who have no record of felonies, substance abuse, or mental illness should have the right to own and carry firearms (including concealed firearms) without the government's permission and with only minimal regulatory requirements (described below).

> ➤ ***Sensible gun control.*** It should be illegal for felons, drug users, and the mentally ill to possess firearms. It should also be illegal for any company or individual to provide a weapon to anybody without a background check. This would require that the government maintain a database of known felons, drug users, and the mentally ill.

> ➤ ***Tasers as an alternative.*** For many citizens, Tasers may provide an effective—and less lethal—alternative to using firearms for self-defense. If more citizens carried them, some mass murders, thefts, and other assaults might be stopped without the danger of killing innocent bystanders.

"This battle for 'common-sense' gun control laws pits emotion and passion against logic and reason. All too often in such a contest, logic loses. So, expect more meaningless, if not harmful, 'gun control' legislation. Good news—if you're a crook." —Libertarian radio commentator Larry Elder

"Gun bans disarm victims, putting them at the mercy of murderers or terrorists who think nothing of breaking the gun laws." —Former radio talk show host Michael Badnarik

"The strongest reason for the people to retain the right to keep and bear arms is, as a last resort, to protect themselves against tyranny in government." —Thomas Jefferson, principle author of the U.S. Declaration of Independence and third president

Religion

"I believe that the Framers of the Constitution made their intent clear when they wrote the First Amendment. I believe they wanted to keep the new government from endorsing one religion over another, not erase the public consciousness or common faith." —Nick Rahall

What's wrong in our battles about religion

- ***Religious intolerance.*** Throughout history, millions of people have been ruthlessly murdered in the name of God. While we can hope for progress, this sort of killing is still taking place in the twenty-first century. It's often a battle over whose God is right. A little more tolerance by all religions would make for a more peaceful world.

- ***Mixing church and state***. England's Magna Carta inspired America's founders to embrace personal liberty, private property, the rule of law, and separation of church and state. There are other nations that don't share these values. In some nations, stoning, prison, or even beheading is condoned for those who do not submit to the state religion.

- ***Laws banning suicide***. One example of mixing church and state in this country are laws that make suicide illegal. It's fine to oppose suicide because of personal or religious values, but why should suicide be illegal in a nation that respects individual liberty? Those laws cause a lot of human suffering as well as unnecessarily increasing medical costs.

- ***Pushing for a US religion***. Some people think the United States should be acknowledged and promoted as a Christian nation because most of the nation's founders were Christian. Many of the founders were quite religious as individuals. However, they didn't want us to drift toward a "state religion." They wanted Americans to be free to make individual choices about religion. They did not want the government to promote *any* religion.

- ***The Christian majority***. Some people argue that America should be a Christian nation because a vast majority of its citizens consider themselves to be Christians. A popular e-mail says the minority should "sit down and shut up." The majority rules, right? Wrong! America's founders were brilliant, and they put a lot of thought into what they created. They didn't give us a pure democracy but rather a democratic constitutional republic. They wanted the government to protect the individual liberties of *every* citizen, not just the majority.

- ***Religious symbolism.*** "In God We Trust" was added to US coins nearly one hundred years after the nation's birth—one of the many things self-serving politicians have done to undermine the incredibly good work of the founders. Adding "under God" to the pledge of allegiance came even later. In both cases, the politicians who did it gained some votes for themselves but damaged our Constitution. As a nation built on a foundation of individual freedom, our choices about God should be individual, private, and personal—not dictated by or even promoted by the government. "In God we trust" should be in your heart if that's your choice, but it should not be on government coins. However...

- ***Over-reaction on both sides***. We waste far too much energy arguing about unimportant religious symbolism. Separation of church and state is important, but banning all displays of religious symbolism in public places is ridiculous. Who is harmed by a manger display at Christmas, the singing of "Hava Nagila," or a discussion of the history of Islam?

How to fix our policies about religion

> ➤ ***Honor the Constitution***. Let individuals make their own choices about religion, and keep the government out of it. (See also the chapter titled "Freedom.")

> ➤ ***Uphold individual liberties***. We shouldn't restrict any individual expression of religious views. Yes, you can erect monuments, send e-mails, put bumper stickers on your cars, and so on. But it isn't individual when the government expresses religious views on our behalf. The government is supposed to represent *all* of us, not just the majority. Let's not forget that difference. And if you're in the majority now, keep in mind that at some time in the future, you could be in the minority. (For more about this point, see the chapter titled "Democracy.")

> ➤ ***Legalize suicide***. In a free society, suicide should be an individual choice. The existing laws drive up medical costs and cause too much human suffering. Just as there should never be laws that force suicide on anyone, we should eliminate laws that make suicide illegal.

➢ ***Focus on the important stuff***. But let's not freak out and waste a lot of energy over symbolism such as coins that proclaim faith in God—especially when there are so many other pressing issues that threaten to send America hurtling off a cliff. Really, shouldn't we be prioritizing issues and talking about things that could actually restore America's greatness? (See also "Congressional Reform," "Deficits," "Education," "Energy and the Environment," "National Security," "Immigration," and "Poverty.")

"I do not feel obliged to believe that the same God who has endowed us with sense, reason, and intellect has intended us to forgo their use." —Italian physicist, astronomer and philosopher Galileo Galilei

"I love you when you bow in your mosque, kneel in your temple, pray in your church. For you and I are sons of one religion, and it is the spirit." —Lebanese-American author Khalil Gibran, author of *The Prophet*

Government

"I don't make jokes...I just watch the government and report the facts." —American cowboy and humorist Will Rogers

"Giving money and power to government is like giving whiskey and car keys to teenage boys." —American humorist P. J. O'Rourke

"Government exists to protect us from each other. Where government has gone beyond its limits is in deciding to protect us from ourselves." —American actor and U.S. President Ronald Reagan

What's wrong with Big Government

- ***There is no such thing as a free government service.*** There's no free lunch, free health care, or free college. Government does not create wealth; individuals do. Governments can only take money from some people and redistribute it to others—and they do an incredibly inefficient job because their ever-expanding bureaucracies take so much off the top.

- ***More government means less freedom.*** America became great because it limited the roles of the federal government, protected individual liberty, and allowed citizens to make their own decisions. We have drifted a long way from those principles. Government is now involved in every facet of our lives. The more powerful and all-encompassing the federal government becomes, the less room there is for the individual initiative and responsibility that made America great.

- ***Governments are inefficient***. Because they have no need to compete, governments generally don't do anything very well. Unlike families and businesses, governments don't have to make good decisions to survive. With the power to tax and impose regulations, they don't have to compete. Without competition, there is little or no pressure to do things better or more efficiently. Here's a challenge for you: try to name even one service or product that the government does a better job providing than the free market.

- ***Government services kill off potential jobs***. When government provides a service or product, it kills businesses, eliminates jobs, stifles competition, and reduces tax revenues—not to mention saddling taxpayers with the higher costs of government bloat, bureaucratic waste, and political corruption.

- ***Government keeps growing.*** Government agencies inevitably become too large and too bureaucratic. Most politicians and bureaucrats believe government is the answer to every problem. That's perfectly natural since it is their chosen field. But government gets even bigger every time somebody demands that politicians "do something" about anything—regardless of whether government can do that something competently or efficiently.

- ***The bigger it gets, the worse it is.*** As institutions become bigger and more powerful, the less likely they are to serve the public interest. This is true of governments, businesses, and special interest groups such as labor unions. Citizens are particularly at risk when Big Government, Big Business, and other big special interest groups cut deals with one another.

- ***Governments always try to do too much.*** Spoiled by generations of government subsidies, beneficiaries always want more. Governments are far too political, with all sorts of special interest groups seeking special favors at the expense of others. Since politicians have no discipline, they agree to take on anything and everything that any campaign contributor requests, regardless of how inappropriate the request is or how many other layers of government are already involved. They overpromise, which is turn causes government to overcommit and underperform.

- **_Government programs never die_**. No matter how badly a government program performs, it is never eliminated. In fact, the tendency is to spend even more taxpayer money to make the program "work better." This is the kind of thinking that only bureaucrats and politicians can afford, and they can afford it only because they are spending other people's (taxpayers) money.

- **_Government employees seldom get fired_**. Government bureaucrats have created work rules that make it impractical to motivate, discipline, or fire incompetent government employees.

- **_Governments attract corruption_**. Power corrupts. Any system that empowers officials to spend other people's money—and allows them to grant favors to themselves and their supporters with that money—is prime breeding territory for corruption. Bigger government logically means bigger temptation for fraud and potential abuse of power by politicians, bureaucrats, government labor unions, and police agencies.

- ***Governments become abusive***. Governments have all the same faults as other big bureaucracies, plus many more. They are especially dangerous because they carry the force of law and are often run by self-righteous ideologues and self-aggrandizing egomaniacs. Self-serving politicians can too easily abuse and misuse their influence.

- ***The dangers of selective enforcement***. Politicians and government bureaucrats—federal, state, and local—create new rules for every possible situation and to cover every single possibility. They are drowning this nation in so many rules that no citizen can possibly know all of them. This means that each of us might unknowingly be in violation of some obscure government regulation. This in turn means that the government could selectively prosecute any citizen who dares to question the government's authority.

- ***Government isn't the solution***. Misguided citizens often demand a government solution for every problem. As their numbers grow, this fundamental error is bringing down the nation. In fact, government is the *cause* of many of our problems. Even well-intentioned government programs are often counterproductive because politicians and bureaucrats can't anticipate the unintended consequences of their actions.

- ***Government caused the financial crisis***. After political meddling, government guarantees, and Wall Street greed caused the artificial housing boom and eventual bust, the same politicians who caused the problem blamed everybody except themselves. (See more about this in "Big Business" and "Economics.")

How to fix Big Government

> ➤ ***Reign in the political class.*** Take away the benefits and financial rewards that politicians have bestowed upon themselves at the public's expense. Limit their power. Limit their ability to reward their cronies. Put the sacrifice and service back into "public service." (See more about this proposal in the chapters "Career Politicians" and "Congressional Reform.")

> ➤ ***Regulatory reform.*** As discussed in the chapter titled "Individual Responsibility," excessive government regulation increases consumer costs, limits choices, and creates new opportunities for influence-peddling and outright fraud by politicians and bureaucrats.

> ➤ ***At-will employment for government employees.*** The complex civil service rules that make it difficult to motivate, discipline, or fire incompetent employees should be replaced by at-will employment (similar to what exists in the private sector). That way, competence would become the best way to gain job security.

> ➤ ***Limited government.*** Recognize how ineffective and inefficient most governments are and carefully define and limit the role of each layer of

government. Limit the federal government's responsibilities to a few well-defined roles, such as national defense, immigration, foreign policy, protection of individual liberties, and the assurance of equal protection under the law. Leave everything else to the state or local governments—or to the people themselves. Hold the federal government accountable for doing a *few* things well, instead of doing *everything* poorly.

➢ ***Keep it small and local***. Always opt for decision making to be made at the lowest or smallest practical level—where individual opinions can be heard, local knowledge is available, bureaucracy can be kept to a minimum, and people are best equipped to recognize political nonsense. Depending on the issue, town solutions are usually more efficient and effective than county solutions, county solutions are preferable to state solutions, and state solutions are preferable to federal solutions.

➢ ***Focus on results***. Most government programs are started with good intentions. Many of them get lousy results, but are almost never eliminated. Instead, politicians and bureaucrats seek to "improve" existing programs by throwing more taxpayer money at them. We should get rid of programs that don't provide results that justify their costs.

> ## *Rein in federal government overreach.*
> Congress has used the "commerce clause" of the Constitution—especially the reference to commerce between the states—to expand the federal government's role far beyond what the nation's founders intended. This has created new opportunities for influence peddling and outright fraud by politicians and bureaucrats. With enough pressure from citizens, Congress could be forced to control itself. If that fails, citizen-driven constitutional amendments may be necessary, as described in the "Take Back Congress" chapter. One of them could be worded something like this: "The Tenth Amendment to the US Constitution *('The powers not delegated to the United States by the Constitution, nor prohibited by it to the States, are reserved to the States respectively, or to the people.')* is reaffirmed, and Article I, Section 8, Clause 3 of the US Constitution *([The Congress shall have Power] 'To regulate Commerce with foreign Nations, and among the several States, and with the Indian tribes')* is amended to delete these words: *'and among the several States.'*"

> ## *Get the government out of the insurance business.* Whenever the government "guarantees" or "insures" anything, it's almost always because no sane person or business will take the risk. Fannie Mae and Freddie Mac, for example, contributed to our housing

bubble and eventual bust and should be eliminated. Flood insurance is another great example: it encourages people (usually rich people) to build where they shouldn't—with the hapless taxpayer covering the predictable losses. Only the government could be this stupid—mainly because the politicians and bureaucrats who make these decisions are spending other people's (taxpayers) money.

> ***Push it down***. The same kind of discipline should be used at other government levels as well. Just because an outcome is desirable doesn't mean that government is the best way to achieve it. If there is a role for government, let it fall to the lowest practical level of government. The smallest government units are closest to the needs of the people and most easily held accountable for results.

> ***Outsource it***. Even when governments have a legitimate role, outsourcing and decentralizing give free markets and competition a chance. Competitive bidding is a great way to make sure the need will be provided as efficiently and effectively as possible. It is important, however, that politicians not be allowed to corrupt the bidding process with political payoffs, crony capitalism, favoritism, and social engineering.

➢ ***Government contract reform.*** Government bids should be subject to free market competition without union-supported politicians saddling taxpayers with the higher cost of government-mandated union wages. (See the "Big Labor" chapter for more about this issue.)

"The best way to understand this whole issue is to look at what the government does: it takes money from some people, keeps a bunch of it, and gives the rest to other people." —American author and columnist Dave Barry

"A government big enough to give you everything you want is strong enough to take everything you have." —Third U.S. President Thomas Jefferson

"Government is the great fiction, through which everybody endeavors to live at the expense of everybody else." —French economist and politician Frederic Bastiat

"Article I, Section 8, of the Constitution, of course, lays out the delegated, enumerated, and therefore limited powers of Congress. Only through a deliberate misreading of the general welfare and commerce clauses of the Constitution has the federal government been allowed to overreach its authority and extend its tendrils into every corner of civil society." —Edward H. Crane, founder of the Cato Institute

Government

"The government is like a baby's alimentary canal: a happy appetite at one end and no responsibility at the other."
—Former U.S. President Ronald Reagan

Energy & the Environment

"Every time I have some moment on a seashore, or in the mountains, or sometimes in a quiet forest, I think this is why the environment has to be preserved." —U.S. Senator Bill Bradley

"Our addiction to foreign oil...is a threat to our national security, and we must address that threat. —U.S. Congressman Jim Costa

What's wrong with America's energy vs. environment stalemate

- ***Energy dependence***. Government regulations against developing America's great energy resources have made the United States dangerously dependent on foreign oil. This undermines our economy. As explained in the "National Security" chapter, our oil dependency also means that we are providing money to terrorists who wish to do us harm.

- ***Environmental concerns.*** We waste far too much time arguing about the science of global warming. Let's focus instead on how much pollution is being dumped into our air, land, and water, which can be measured objectively. The world needs to find ways to treat Mother Earth more gently. But it is also obvious that some overzealous environmental regulations are threatening our national security and hurting the economy.

- ***Fickle consumers***. Consumers find ways to use less energy when prices are high. Gasoline prices are a great example. When gas prices are high, people tend to buy more fuel-efficient vehicles and are more willing to consider alternative fuel vehicles. They make more use of carpooling and public transportation. They are more likely to try to live closer to their workplaces, vacation closer to home, and inquire about work-from-home options. Yet they tend to return to their old behaviors once gasoline prices go down.

- ***Political stalemate.*** America has become more environmentally aware, but our conflicting desires for a great standard of living with lots of conveniences *and* a cleaner environment have created political gridlock.

How to fix our energy and environment policies

> ➢ ***Energy independence.*** The economy and our national security should be our top short-term priorities. We simply can't remain as dependent as we are on unstable or unfriendly foreign nations. We must relax some of the environmental regulations that are preventing us from developing our own proven sources of energy. Doing this now would also be a powerful economic stimulus at a time when we desperately need one.

> ➢ ***Tax pollution instead of regulating it.*** The environment must be a key long-term priority. Government's environmental regulations are costly to administer and are harming our economy and national security. Imposing higher consumer taxes on energy sources that pollute would be a more efficient and effective way to help the environment in the long-term.

> ➢ ***Consumer impact of taxing pollution.*** If consumers knew, for example, that gasoline taxes will increase by ten cents a gallon every three months for the next ten years, they would find ways to reduce their consumption, permanently

making many of the adjustments mentioned earlier in this chapter.

➤ ***Business impact of taxing pollution***. If businesses knew that national policy will be to steadily increase taxation to battle pollution, they would produce the energy we need short-term while also developing cleaner energy sources for the future. As taxes on pollution steadily increase, alternative energy sources will become increasingly viable and the incentives to develop alternatives will become stronger.

➤ ***A gentle transition***. Gradually phasing in these pollution taxes would allow consumers and businesses to make the necessary adjustments without undue harm to the economy. The income from these taxes would also allow the government to reduce other taxes as well as reducing deficit spending and the national debt.

"We need to raise gasoline and carbon taxes to discourage their use and drive the creation of a new clean energy industry, while we cut payroll and corporate taxes to encourage employment and domestic investment." —New York Times *columnist Thomas Friedman*

"Liberals in Congress have spent the past three decades pandering to environmental extremists. The policies they have put in place are in large part responsible for the energy crunch

we are seeing today. We have not built a refinery in this country for 30 years." —U.S. Representative Marsha Blackburn

Immigration

"Ours is an open and accepting society, and has historically provided an avenue for lawful immigration to all those willing to accept the responsibilities of citizenship." —U.S. Representative Spencer Bachus

"Illegal immigration is crisis for our country. It is an open door for drugs, criminals, and potential terrorists to enter our country. It is straining our economy, adding costs to our judicial, healthcare, and education systems." —U.S. Representative. Timothy Murphy

What's wrong with America's immigration policies

- ***Legal immigrants made America great***. Millions of immigrants came to America (legally) because they were free to work as hard as they wished, free to enjoy the fruits of their labor, free to make their own decisions, and willing to live with the consequences of their own decisions. America was a place where everybody could control his or her own destiny. And that's why the nation—fueled by all those hardworking immigrants—thrived.

- ***The federal government has botched immigration***. Immigration policy and enforcement are among the few functions that should clearly be the responsibility of the federal government. One again, Congress and federal bureaucrats have proven that they don't do anything very well.

- **_Selective enforcement_**. It's dangerous to pass laws and then ignore them. Selective enforcement provides too many opportunities for government favoritism, fraud, and abuse. But that's precisely what the government has done—for many decades—with our immigration laws. It can't even do a decent job of keeping track of people who overstay their visas.

- **_We enticed people to disobey our immigration laws_**. Illegal immigration has been an accepted part of the American economy for decades. Our farmers needed cheap labor, so government ignored our immigration laws and welcomed illegal immigrants with a wink and a nod (and, in many cases, government benefits too).

- **_Which laws count and which don't?_** Passing unrealistic laws or failing to enforce them leads to a general disregard for the need to obey laws. If we don't enforce our immigration laws and employers disregard these laws in their hiring practices, how long before mainstream society starts ignoring other laws, cheating on taxes, and so on?

- ***Knee-jerk positions***. Those who ask "What is it about 'illegal' that you don't understand"? are absolutely correct—just as correct as those who argue that it would be morally and economically disastrous to break up families and deport millions of people who were enticed here and have become valued and contributing members of our society.

How to fix America's immigration policies

> *__Tighter border security__*. For national security, terrorist prevention, and economic reasons, the federal government must do a better job securing our borders. We can do this with better use of technology as well as by bringing more troops home from our unnecessary outposts around the world. (See more about this in the "National Security" chapter.)

> *__Remove incentives for illegal immigration.__* Because of misguided government policies and lax enforcement, there are far too many incentives for people to enter the country illegally or to overstay their visas. Federal and state governments must do a better job of eliminating these incentives. It makes no sense that illegal immigrations are eligible for government benefits or that anybody born in the United States should be eligible for citizenship even if the parents are in the country illegally. Electronic verification of legal status as a condition of employment is a worthwhile system.

> *__We can be choosy__*. If we can retain the things that made America great, we will always have more people wanting in

than the country can absorb. So we can—and should—be choosy about who gets in. Our immigration laws should therefore be based on what's good for America instead of on "political correctness or lotteries. The immigrants we accept for work permits should be those who have skills our nation needs, as proven by a legitimate job offer. To be considered for citizenship, an immigrant should first demonstrate the ability to be economically self-sufficient, as well as mastery of the English language and an understanding of American history and American values.

➢ ***Work permits, not citizenship, for those already here***. Long-time illegal immigrants who have otherwise been law-abiding and are gainfully employed and self-sufficient should be granted work permits but not citizenship. Work permits would be an acknowledgment that the federal government—with its misguided policies and "nod and wink" lack of enforcement—induced many immigrants to enter the country illegally and/or to overstay their visas.

"A simple way to take measure of a country is to look at how many want in. And how many want out." —British Prime Minister Tony Blair

Deficit Spending

"The budget should be balanced, the Treasury should be refilled, public debt should be reduced, the arrogance of officialdom should be tempered and controlled, and the assistance to foreign lands should be curtailed lest Rome become bankrupt. People must again learn to work, instead of living on public assistance." —Attributed to Cicero, 55 BC

"Imagine this family budget: Last year, you earned $24,700. But you spent $37,900, incurring $13,300 in debt, and you were already $153,500 in debt. So you say, "I promise I'll spend $300 less this year!" Anyone can see that your cutback is pathetic and that you need to spend *much* less. Yet if you add eight zeroes, that's America's budget." —American author and columnist John Stossel

What's wrong with deficit spending

- ***Deficits matter.*** The experts have claimed that government deficits don't matter. This is self-serving hogwash from the elite political class. Every citizen with an ounce of common sense knows that you can't spend more than you earn and that you can borrow money only if you will be able to repay it. Only those in government—blinded by their ability to print money, devalue the dollar with inflation, and still get reelected—haven't grasped these elementary facts.

- **_Federal spending is out of control_.** In the Great Depression year of 1934, federal spending as a percentage of the Gross National Product (GNP) topped 10 percent for the first time. This was mainly because of President Roosevelt's well-intentioned but misguided New Deal economic controls, regulations, and spending—which ended up deepening and prolonging the depression. Federal spending reached 12 percent of the GNP during World War II. Today federal spending is approaching 25 percent of the GNP—and Democrats and Republicans are resisting efforts to reduce spending significantly.

- **_Federal inefficiency_.** The federal government doesn't do anything very well or very efficiently. It takes money out of the economy via taxation, ships it to Washington, spends a lot of it on inefficient bureaucracies, and then sends what's left back to other governments with so many mandates that more money is wasted before anything actually happens. State and local governments would do a much better job filling state and local needs without this kind of "help" from the federal government. (See more about this in the "Government" and "Poverty" chapters.)

- ***Government is the problem.*** Not only is government spending not the solution to our problems, it is the cause of many of them. As discussed in the "Government" chapter, even well-intentioned government programs are often counterproductive because politicians and bureaucrats can't anticipate—or don't understand—the unintended consequences of their actions.

- ***Government dependency.*** Because America has been so successful, citizens increasingly feel entitled to America's blessings without doing anything to earn them. A growing number of voters are dependent on the government and believe it is the government's job to take care of them. This is an addiction and one that won't be easy to rehab.

- ***Political promises.*** When people expect the government to take care of them, they tend to elect the politicians who make the biggest promises. Those politicians surround themselves with staffers (paid by taxpayers) whose only goal is to ensure the reelection of their boss. Voters like to have things provided to them free, so politicians offer more government services and lower taxes: a fatal combination for any nation.

- ***Taxpayers are victims***. The requirement that companies seeking government contracts must (in effect) pay union wages and often follow union rules shuts out the more flexible and more efficient smaller businesses—and taxpayers therefore pay more than is necessary for almost everything government does. (See the "Big Labor" chapter for more about this issue.)

- ***Government can't create wealth***. Regardless of the promises made by career politicians, government can't create wealth. Government can take wealth from some citizens to give it to others, but doing so penalizes producers, makes non-producers increasingly dependent on the government, encourages class warfare, and leads to eventual collapse.

- ***Political gridlock***. As usual, both parties are wrong: Democrats for avoiding spending reform (to please their Big Labor supporters) and Republicans for avoiding tax reform (to please their Big Business supporters). In addition, both parties have tolerated deficit spending and irresponsible borrowing.

How to fix our deficit spending

> ➤ *__Get rid of career politicians__*. Capping their pay and eliminating their pensions would be good first steps. (See the "Career Politicians" chapter for more details about this proposal.)

> ➤ *__Limit the roles of the federal government__*. Hold the federal government accountable for doing a *few* things well instead of trying to do everything (and doing *everything* poorly). (See more about this in the "Government" chapter.)

> ➤ *__Stop federal funding for state and local projects__*. It makes no sense for the federal government to dole out money for state and local projects. The federal government should provide funding only for legitimate *federal* needs, just as state and local governments should provide funding only for legitimate *state* and *local* needs. Let the people closest to those needs make the decisions. (See "Government" for more information.)

> ➤ *__Stop welfare for businesses__*. As explained in the chapters "Big Business" and "Taxes," phase out tax loopholes and government payments to businesses.

➢ ***Cut the costs of crime, courts, and prisons.*** As explained in the "Crime, Courts, and Prisons" chapter, legalize drug use and victimless crimes, rein in greedy lawyers, streamline courts, and make prisoners pay their own way.

➢ ***Get control of entitlements***: As explained in the "Entitlements" chapter, gradually increase the age at which people can start drawing Social Security and Medicare benefits, and give people a chance to opt out of the benefits.

➢ ***Get the government out of the insurance business***. Whenever the government guarantees or insures anything, it's almost always because no sane person or business will take the risk. (See more about this point in the "Government" chapter.)

➢ ***Fund students instead of bureaucracies***. With public education, we spend a lot of money for dismal results. Get government out of the way, provide funding to students instead of bureaucrats, and let consumers make their own choices in a free market. (See more about this in the "Education.")

➢ ***Help the poor instead of enslaving them***. Since the federal government has made poverty more widespread and enduring, all federal welfare programs should be phased out and replaced by a negative income tax. (See the "Poverty" chapter for more details about how the negative income tax would work.)

> ***Government contract reform***. Government bids should be subject to free market competition, without union-supported politicians saddling taxpayers with the higher cost of government-mandated union wages. (Also see the "Big Labor" chapter.)

> ***Stop being the world's bank and policeman***. Stop trying to buy friends with foreign aid (especially to corrupt governments), let other nations fight their own battles without putting our boots on their streets, use our technology instead of our troops to defend ourselves and our friends, maintain a strong (but tactical and efficient) military, and react intelligently to the threat of terrorism. (Also see the "National Security" chapter.)

"The powers not delegated to the United States by the Constitution, nor prohibited by it to the States, are reserved to the States respectively, or to the people." —Tenth Amendment to the US Constitution

Crime, Courts & Prisons

"We used to be a free people. Now we are hedged in by millions of laws. Harassed by a plague of opportunistic lawyers. Harmed by regulations meant for our protection. Unnecessarily taxed to pay for a suffocating bureaucracy. Drowning in petty paperwork. Stifled by 'rights' that rarely benefit anyone." —American journalist Joan Beck

What's wrong with our crime, courts, and prison policies

- ***Expensive, cumbersome, and overloaded courts***. Justice happens too slowly and costs too much. Courts and jails are often overloaded and bogged down by victimless crimes (such as drug use and prostitution), self-serving lawyers, and endless appeals.

- ***The government's war on drugs has been a gigantic failure***. We are reliving—on an even bigger and more tragic scale—this nation's horrible experiment with Prohibition. That's when the federal government outlawed alcohol—thus creating huge crime problems and wasting precious resources trying unsuccessfully to enforce an unenforceable law. Legalizing alcohol allowed us to control and tax it. We still have some alcoholics, but plenty of nonprofit and nongovernment services are available to help alcoholics and their victims.

- **_Greedy lawyers_**. As mentioned in the "Health Care" chapter, lawyers have distorted a great American justice system beyond recognition. It's no longer about justice but rather about how lawyers can become richer at the expense of the rest of society.

- **_Ineffective prisons_**. Too many people who go to prison come out with improved criminal skills and have to be imprisoned again later. Too few are prepared to return to society as contributing and law-abiding citizens.

- **_Taxpayers are the victims_**. Taxpayers ultimately pay for the endless misuse of our court system. They provide the courts, judges, prosecutors, and administrators that allow the lawyers to game the system at taxpayer expense.

How to fix our crime, courts, and prison policies

> **_People's courts (no-lawyers-allowed)._**
> Cities, counties, and states could create
> "people's courts" in which many cases
> could be heard without any lawyers
> being involved. Civil (noncriminal) cases
> that involve disputes between individuals
> or companies would be especially
> appropriate for this system. The judges
> could be nonlawyers who are more
> concerned with real justice than legal
> complexities. Their assignment could be
> to propose solutions that are fair to both
> parties. Some trials could be conducted
> via e-mail at minimal expense. Losers
> could still have the right to appeal.

> **_Loser pays._** People would be a lot more
> cautious about suing one another—and
> a lot more willing to compromise or
> accept people's court decisions—if losers
> had to bear the cost of the litigation.
> These costs could include the cost of
> judges, juries, and administrators (why
> should taxpayers bear these expenses in
> private disputes?) as well as the winner's
> reasonable lawyer fees.

> **_Limit damages._** States can set
> reasonable limits on damages that can
> be awarded in civil cases, including

malpractice suits. (See the "Health Care" chapter for more about this proposal.)

> ***Streamline court processes***. Many trials could be conducted by judges or smaller juries. Evidence and testimony could be submitted in writing and made available in advance to both sides and to judges and jurors, thus dramatically reducing the amount of time it takes to conduct the trial and reach a verdict. Many trials could be "virtual" to save time and energy as well as reducing legal and court costs.

> ***Reduce red tape and regulations***. One of the reasons people turn to crime is that it is too difficult to earn a living legally because of government regulations. Minimum wage laws reduce the number of entry-level jobs, making it hard for low-skilled people to start the climb up the economic ladder. Hundreds of occupations require bureaucrat red tape and a government license. You need permission from an astounding number of government agencies to start a business, drive a cab, become a hairdresser, braid hair, polish nails, shine shoes, scalp tickets or sell trinkets from a pushcart. For some people, crime is simply easier than going through all the red tape.

> ***Legalize victimless crimes***. Just because we think something is bad doesn't mean it should be illegal. In a truly free society, government should not try to dictate morality. Prostitution, for example, is illegal even when it occurs between two willing adults. The fact that it is illegal drives it underground, creates black markets, enables pimps, and overburdens our police, courts, and jails. And why should suicide be illegal if we are truly free people?

> ***End the drug war***. It's time to recognize that freedom includes the right to self-destruct. Ending the war on drugs would pay huge benefits to our society. Legalizing, controlling, and taxing drugs would reduce the cost of drugs and the profit motive of criminal drug dealers. It would unburden our overloaded police, courts, and jails. The reduced costs and new tax revenues would help eliminate the government's deficit spending too.

> ***Eliminate the death penalty***. It is dangerous to give any government the power to kill its own citizens. Courts make mistakes, the justice system isn't perfect, and the death penalty can never be taken back. In addition, the death penalty is often more costly to society than a sentence of life in prison because of the costs of litigation and the decades of appeals.

➤ **_Reduce the cost of law enforcement_**. We can reduce costs dramatically by legalizing victimless crimes, ending the war on drugs, eliminating the death penalty, and using alternative punishments (such as electronic house arrest) instead of prisons for nonviolent criminals.

➤ **_Negative income tax_**. Poverty is a major reason for crime. The federal government should replace all its failing poverty programs with a brilliantly simple negative income tax. (See the "Poverty" chapter for more details about this proposal.)

➤ **_Make prisoners work and pay_**. Law-abiding taxpayers should not be burdened with the cost of punishing criminals. Prisoners should be required to work to pay for their own food, lodging, health care, and privileges (such as television viewing or time outside their cells). Whenever practical, the work made available to inmates could include elements of job training. Those who refuse to work would be making a free choice, and they would be responsible for the consequences. What better way to prepare them for a return to the real world?

"When there aren't enough criminals, one makes them. One declares so many things to be a crime that it becomes impossible for men to live without breaking laws." —Ayn Rand, author, *Atlas Shrugged*

"Legalizing drugs would simultaneously reduce the amount of crime and also raise the quality of law enforcement. Can you conceive of any other measure that would accomplish so much to promote law and order?" —Milton Friedman, economist and author

Entitlements

"For more than forty years, the United States Congress has shamelessly used payroll taxes intended for Social Security to fund big government spending." -- —Mike Pence.

What's wrong with our entitlement policies

- ***Cruel government hoax.*** Social Security and many other government entitlement programs are legal only because the government runs them. Jane and Juan Q. Citizen are forced to pay into Social Security, with the implied promise that the money is being invested for their retirement. It's a hoax perpetuated by career politicians and bureaucrats. Instead of investing Jane and Juan's money, the government uses it to pay people who have already retired. Even when there are more people paying in than retired people drawing benefits, the politicians spend the surpluses on more government programs. The attitude of these thieves of the public's money (who, laughably, call themselves "public servants") was, "*We can use their money to buy their votes with more promises and more spending, so why not?*" And for too long, citizens allowed them to get away with it because we either didn't understand or didn't want to face up to it.

- ***It's unsustainable***. Social Security worked well when there were plenty of working people paying into it and not as many retirees. Well, the jig is up. Now that baby boomers are retiring, there are more people retiring and fewer working people to support them. Plus people are living longer. So the Ponzi scheme called Social Security is unsustainable.

- ***Medicare***. Another significant unsustainable entitlement, Medicare, is discussed in the chapter titled "Health Care."

How to fix our entitlements mess

> ***Take back our money.*** The *taxpayer-funded* portion of congressional retirement accounts should be put into the general Social Security fund. (See the "Career Politicians" chapter for more about this proposal.)

> ***Retire later.*** People are living longer and there won't be enough money to support all those baby boomers in retirement. In order to ensure enough money will be there to meet our long-term obligations, we must gradually increase the age at which Social Security can be drawn. (See "Poverty" to consider how a negative income tax could help ease the long wait for the truly needy.)

> ***Broaden and lower the Social Security tax***. The first $106,800 in income is currently taxed 4.2 percent for Society Security; the portion of an individual's income over $106,800 is not subject to this tax. Applying the payroll tax to all income would allow a reduction in the 4.2 percent rate. This would be an overdue admission that Social Security is a massive income distribution/welfare system (NOT a retirement investment).

> ***Phase it out.*** The three steps above—especially the second and third

steps—would solve Social Security's short-term financial problem without undue hardship to anybody. Once the system is on sound financial footing, new workers not already paying into Social Security should not be forced to do so. They would be better off investing in their own retirement plans. The government isn't good at this sort of thing anyway, and Social Security would end naturally when the last retiree already in the system dies.

> ***Let people opt out.*** Finally, workers already in the system could be permitted to opt out of Social Security entirely under carefully conceived conditions. Those who have already put money in could choose either a one-time cash transfer to their private retirement account (IRA or 401k) or reduced Social Security benefits when they retire. (Structured properly so the system wouldn't end up with too few contributors to cover payments, this could be a win-win situation for these individuals *and* for the stability of Social Security.)

> ***Means testing***. Even after the steps mentioned above, means testing may still be necessary to meet our Social Security obligations. People who are successful enough to be able to retire comfortably without drawing Social

Security may have to have their future
benefits reduced or eliminated.
Reductions could be on a sliding scale
based on income.

"For my children, it makes sense to talk about modernizing
Social Security, letting them create stronger personal
accounts, letting them get a higher rate of return over the
long run." —U.S. Senator John Sununu

Taxes

"I contend that for a nation to try to tax itself into prosperity is like a man standing in a bucket and trying to lift himself up by the handle." —British Prime Minister Winston Churchill

"Politicians never accuse you of 'greed' for wanting other people's money—only for wanting to keep your own money." —American journalist Joseph Sobran

"Manipulating taxes to favor or disfavor particular industries, groups or regions is a source of power that Democrats and Republicans alike are loath to surrender. That's why major tax reform fails, despite routine endorsements from both parties." —American journalist Robert Samuelson

What's wrong with our tax policies

- ***Citizen distrust***. The federal tax code is so complicated and full of loopholes that the typical citizen can't even file a tax return without expert help. This creates a drag on the economy due to the thousands of accounting and tax jobs that would otherwise be unnecessary. It also requires huge federal bureaucracies—paid for by taxpayers—to monitor and enforce compliance. Most important, this system undermines the trust in government that is so important in a free society and encourages class warfare.

- **_Political corruption_**. Instead of setting tax policies that are good for the economy (and therefore good for the people), politicians use tax policy to favor their friends and punish their enemies. "Elections have consequences" usually means that Big Business is favored when Republicans are in power, and Big Labor is favored when Democrats are in power.

- **_Corporate tax loopholes_**. The 35 percent federal corporate tax rate is too high, but it's a misleading statistic. Only about 25 percent of corporations actually pay 30 percent or more; another 25 percent pay 10 percent or less or get money back because of loopholes and tax credits. These statistics show how broken the system is thanks to our politicians, Big Business lobbyists, and their loopholes and tax credits.

- **_High tax rates hurt the middle class_**. Higher tax rates hurt the middle class most—especially consumers and small businesses—because big businesses can move their investments to foreign countries with lower tax rates when our tax rates are too high.

- **_Class warfare_**. Democrat demagogues incite fears and encourage class warfare with their calls to "tax the rich"; Republican demagogues do the same with their railing against welfare recipients and their calls for "no tax increases." Both positions are irrational. Citizens must be smart enough to see through the politicians who talk this kind of nonsense.

- **_No tax increases?_** Republicans who have signed the "no tax increases" pledge are fiscally irresponsible and politically dishonest. The government can't continue to spend 25+ percent more every year than it takes in—any more than a family can—without soon facing bankruptcy.

- **_Tax the rich?_** Democrats who argue that taxing the rich will solve the nation's deficit spending are fiscally irresponsible and politically dishonest. If the government imposed a 100 percent tax rate on all income over $250,000 annually, it would only cover 141 days of government spending—with nothing left for the other 224 days of the year. And that's assuming that none of the rich individuals flee the country to avoid the 100 percent tax rate; obviously, many would leave. Taxing the rich won't solve the problem; it's just a way for dishonest politicians to dupe gullible voters and avoid facing up to our nation's spending problem.

- ***Deficit spending***. Deficit spending and excessive borrowing hurt the economy, weaken the dollar, and undermine the economy. Only governments think they can get away with spending more money than they have—and it can't work for them over the long haul either.

How to fix our tax policies

> ***Get spending under control.*** Once we remove the career politicians, we'll be able to limit the roles and spending of government. (See the chapters titled "Career Politicians," "Election Reform," "Deficits," "Entitlements," "National Security," and "Poverty.")

> ***Simplify taxes to build trust and stop political mischief.*** Freedom is at stake when the income tax code is so complicated that the typical citizen can't understand it. Complicated tax structures open the door to political mischief, special interest lobbying, class warfare, and citizen distrust. All loopholes and deductions should be phased out, with the exception of charitable deductions; this would allow lower tax rates to be phased in. (Gently phasing in these changes is important to avoid disruptions.)

> ***One-size-fits-all flat income tax rate.*** What could be fairer than a flat tax rate that applies equally to all personal income, including capital gains? A 10–15 percent income tax rate should suffice once spending is under control and loopholes are phased out. People wouldn't pay any income taxes at all on the minimal amount that qualifies them

for the negative income tax (as described in the "Poverty" chapter). On all income above that minimum amount, we would all pay the same percentage. The more you earn, the more you'd pay—but the percentage would be the same for everyone above the poverty level.

> ***Globally competitive taxes***. We live in a global society in the twenty-first century, so tax policies and tax rates must be competitive with those in other countries. The smart thing is to make sure our taxes (on the whole) are competitive globally in order to encourage investment in America. This should always be possible if we don't overspend or engage in political gamesmanship.

> ***Tax consistency***. Businesses and consumers hate uncertainty, and uncertainty weakens the economy. (See more about this point in the "Economics" chapter). Consistent and competitive tax rates and policies would ensure a vigorous economy and therefore provide the government with a reasonably consistent flow of tax revenues. If combined with reasonable government spending, we would have balanced budgets.

➢ ***Corporate tax reform***. Get rid of the corporate tax code that puts smaller businesses at a huge disadvantage when competing with larger businesses. Substitute simplified business taxes that won't require armies of accountants and tax consultants. US corporations should be taxed on their worldwide income, with credits for taxes paid in foreign countries. But the corporate income tax rates must be competitive globally so companies won't be so motivated to park their offshore earnings in other countries.

➢ ***Progressive corporate income taxes***. Introduce progressive corporate income tax rates. Smaller companies might pay very low corporate income taxes, but the tax rate would gradually become higher as the company grows. This would discourage monopolies and encourage the voluntary breakup of huge companies into smaller (not "too big to fail") companies. (See the "Big Business" chapter for the reasoning behind this proposal.)

➢ ***Stop the crony capitalism tax breaks***. The government should stop giving special tax breaks to selected industries. Special breaks simply open the door for more lobbying by big companies and more payoffs to politicians.

➤ **_Tax pollution instead of regulating it_**. As explained in the "Energy" chapter, imposing higher consumer taxes on energy sources that pollute would be a more efficient and effective way to help the environment long-term.

➤ **_Legalize, control, and tax drugs_**. As explained in "Crime," ending the war on drugs would bring huge benefits to our society. The new tax revenues would help eliminate government's deficit spending too.

➤ **_Stop the class warfare_**. Citizens need to be smart enough to expose and condemn politicians who incite class warfare over tax policy. The top 20 percent of earners pay 85 percent of all income taxes, and that's okay. Most successful people don't mind paying more taxes than the less successful as long as the system has integrity and overall tax policy is competitive globally. Broader and lower taxes, along with phasing out tax deductions and special interest loopholes, would restore integrity and consistency to the tax system.

➤ **_Negative income tax_**. The federal government should replace all its failing poverty programs with a brilliantly simple negative income tax. This would be the best way to avoid the class warfare toward which the nation seems to be careening. (See the "Poverty" chapter for more details about how the negative income tax would work.)

"The only difference between a tax man and a taxidermist is that the taxidermist leaves the skin." —American author and humorist Mark Twain

"[The IRS's] contempt for citizens...is so routine, and so unlimited, that the agency has become a kind of Frankenstein, running wild and terrorizing Americans at will. The IRS hypocritically requires mistake-free returns when its own books are in shambles. It demands exorbitant sums of money without regard to the accuracy of its claims. It doesn't hesitate to use every possible maneuver to get what it wants, sometimes destroying businesses—and lives—in the process." —Libertarian author James Bovard

"As I went about with my father, when he collected taxes, I knew that when taxes were laid someone had to work hard to earn the money to pay them." —30th U.S. President Calvin Coolidge

Democracy or Republic?

"Democracy must be something more than two wolves and a sheep voting on what to have for dinner." —James Bovard

What's wrong with democracy

- ***Pure democracy doesn't work—and never has.*** One of the biggest mistakes this country has made is to promote the idea of democracy to the rest of the world. Nations that opt for democracy without granting and protecting individual freedoms are doomed to chaos and eventual failure.

- ***Mob rule vs. individual rights***. Democracy is nothing more than mob rule, so we're darned lucky that's not what this nation's founders gave us. They instead gave us a constitutional republic that grants individual liberty to its citizens and pledges the nation to defend those liberties above all else. They wisely warned, "If you can keep it." It's ours to preserve and protect—or to lose.

- ***Government rulers vs. individual liberty***. The founders knew that the greatest threats to individual liberty would come from the government itself, so they also carefully limited the power and scope of the federal government. It is important to remember that equal opportunity for all does not mean equal results for all. Freedom means every individual is free to succeed...as well as being free to fail.

- ***We're forfeiting our heritage***. Unfortunately these lessons have been lost on future generations. Our government promotes democracy to the rest of the world. And the commerce clause of the Constitution has been used as an excuse for the federal government to get involved in all facets of American life—at great harm to the nation and its future.

How to fix our Democratic Republic

> ➤ **_Educate our citizens_**. Our own citizens—including our political leaders and teachers—need a better understanding of the important differences between pure democracies and constitutional republics, as well as the dangers of mob rule and oppressive governments. If we are too lazy to pay attention, America's decline and eventual collapse are inevitable. (See also the "Education," "Government," and "Freedom" chapters.)

> ➤ **_Promote liberty worldwide_**. The United States must promote the importance of individual liberty and equal opportunity—not just democracy or equal outcomes—to the rest of the world. The best influence we could have on other countries would be to set a good example here at home. (See the "Religion" chapter for comments about the importance of separation of church and state.)

> ➤ **_Limit government power_**. Restrict the federal government to the roles specified in the Constitution. Return everything else to the people, and allow them to decide which other functions should be performed by their local and state governments. With strict limits on the role of government, there will be less money for politicians to give away and

fewer favors that can be granted to cronies or denied to the enemies of cronies. (See the "Government" chapter for more about the importance of limiting the role of government.)

➤ **_Election reform_**. Only individuals should be allowed to make campaign contributions to politicians. Campaign contributions by special interest groups should not be permitted. (Also see the "Election Reform" chapter.)

➤ **_Rein in career politicians_**. Capping pay and eliminating pensions for elected officials, as well as limiting their power, would help rein in the career politicians. (Also see the "Career Politicians" chapter.)

"The framers held democracy and majority rule in deep contempt. As a matter of fact, the term democracy appears in none of our founding documents. James Madison argued that 'measures are too often decided, not according to the rules of justice and the rights of the minor party, but by the superior force of an interested and overbearing majority.' John Adams said: 'Remember, democracy never lasts long. It soon wastes, exhausts and murders itself. There never was a democracy yet that did not commit suicide.'—American columnist Walter Williams

National Security

"The moral and constitutional obligations of our representatives in Washington are to protect our liberty—not coddle the world, precipitating no-win wars, while bringing bankruptcy and economic turmoil to our people." —U.S. Representative Ron Paul

"A politician is a fellow who will lay down your life for his country." —Texas Guinan, American saloon keeper and actress

What's wrong with our national security policies

- ***The world is becoming more dangerous.*** While we hope for—and should continue to work toward—world peace, we should remember that the world has always suffered from conflict. We have always had ignorance, religious and racial intolerance, and ruthless dictators. Now we also have frighteningly powerful and sophisticated weaponry—and it appears unlikely that we will be able to keep these weapons out of the hands of terrorists and other maniacs. This is especially true because our own energy dependence results in us providing funding for many of those terrorist groups. Cyber-terrorism may be the next huge threat.

- ***Policing the entire world?*** For too long, America has tried to serve as the world's policeman. We once were known for "speaking softly but carrying a big stick," but our voice has become shrill, we have become far too quick to use our military might, and we've tried to use foreign aid to buy friends or prop up dictators. In too much of the world, we are feared, distrusted, and played for the fool rather than respected.

- ***Military aggression***. The service of our military forces has always been a source of pride. Our noble history was that we didn't start wars, but we would rise to the occasion if attacked. In recent years, we've been far too willing to be the aggressor in the hope that we can proactively eliminate real or perceived threats. This has come at great cost in loss of lives, casualties for families, diminished prestige around the world, and the financial burden on taxpayers.

- ***Either/or thinking***. The military-industrial complex has too often dismissed as unpatriotic any effort to restrain military spending: in their minds you are either a "hawk" or you are un-American. This is nonsense. We can and must make intelligent choices that will keep us strong without funding every military request—and our military leaders are entirely capable of making the right choices.

- ***Terrorism vs. liberty***. The fear of terrorism has caused us to forfeit too many individual liberties at home, to grant far too much power to the government, and to burden our economy with far too much regulation and spending. Because terrorists have occasionally used airplanes, we have made commercial airline travel almost intolerable. Yet even though most terrorists are Arabs, our political correctness prevents us from the racial profiling that could actually make airplane travel far safer—and do it far more efficiently.

How to fix America's national security policies

> ➤ ***Keep a strong military.*** It is vital that we retain sufficient military power to deter attacks on ourselves and our friends. The concept of "mutually assured destruction" prevented outright war during our standoff with the Soviet Union: each country knew that the other had the power to blow them off the face of the earth. For the foreseeable future, the fear of mutually assured destruction may be the world's best chance for peace.

> ➤ ***Make it a tactical military.*** We can and must make intelligent tactical choices that will keep us strong without funding every request from the Pentagon and its military contractors. If national defense is our mission, it doesn't mean that we must maintain superiority in every possible weapon. And it wouldn't be unpatriotic to stop the waste and fraud that claim billions of our tax dollars every year and instead invest some of it in developing the capacity to defend ourselves against the cyber-terrorism attacks that surely lie ahead. If we challenge our military leaders to live within a sensible budget, they are entirely capable of making good choices.

➢ **_Use our technology, not our troops_**. It's dumb for us to be fighting wars in the twenty-first century essentially the same way we did in previous centuries. Given our mastery of military technology, there should never again be a need for us to send American ground troops to fight wars outside our own borders. When we feel compelled to help people in another country, we can provide technical support and let them provide the ground troops. Send in the drones, but not the troops!

➢ **_Stop policing the entire world_**. Even if we could be successful at it, we simply can't continue to police the entire world. The cost is just too high in terms of human lives and the impact on our struggling economy. America should always do its share, but that shouldn't include us keeping American troops in over 120 countries.

➢ **_Phase out foreign aid._** The best way we can influence the rest of the world is by providing a great example of how freedom, tolerance, and limited government can lead to prosperity. No country spends as much on foreign aid and gets so little in return. We often cause harm by propping up dictators around the world. We can't pay our own bills. Our addiction to deficit spending is destroying our economy. (See also the

"Economics," "Freedom," and "Poverty" chapters.)

➤ ***Stop funding terrorism***. As explained in the "Energy" chapter, government regulations have made the United States dangerously dependent on foreign oil and vulnerable to foreign governments that don't share our values. It also means that we are providing funding to terrorists who wish to do us harm, as well as undermining our own economy.

➤ ***Stop our irrational fear of terrorism.*** Acts of terrorism get a lot of attention because they are so dramatic and so deplorable. The attacks of 9/11 were tragic, but too many Americans—and especially our government—have overreacted. You are more likely to die in an auto accident or from old age than you are from an act of terrorism. So let's take practical steps to minimize terrorism—including doing a much better job of defending ourselves from cyber terrorism attacks—but let's not sacrifice our liberty and undermine our economy.

➤ ***Promote liberty worldwide***. The United States must promote the importance of individual rights and the separation of church and state—not just democracy—to the rest of the world. This means equal rights for every person but no special privileges for anyone. The best influence we could have on other nations would be to set a good example here at home. (See the "Freedom," "Democracy," and "Religion" chapters for more about this point.)

"Foreign aid might be defined as a transfer of money from poor people in rich countries to rich people in poor countries."—American economist Douglas Casey

"Terrorism is the war of the poor. War is the terrorism of the rich." —American novelist Leon Uris

"The average taxpayer in Germany or Japan pays less for the defense of his country than the average taxpayer in America pays for the defense of Germany or Japan." —1984 Libertarian Party candidate for U.S. President David Bergland

"We need to get out of Afghanistan—even if it entails risks—because we can't afford to spend $190 million a day to bring its corrupt warlords from the 15th to the 19th century." —Columnist and author Thomas Friedman

Economics

"Only when the human spirit is allowed to invent and create, only when individuals are given a personal stake in deciding economic policies and benefiting from their success—only then can societies remain economically alive, dynamic, prosperous, progressive and free." —Former U.S. President Ronald Reagan

"The key insight of Adam Smith's *Wealth of Nations* is misleadingly simple: if an exchange between two parties is voluntary, it will not take place unless both believe they will benefit from it. Most economic fallacies derive from the neglect of this simple insight, from the tendency to assume that there is a fixed pie, that one party can gain only at the expense of another." —Milton Friedman, Nobel Prize-winning economist, and author of *Free to Choose*

Too few Americans understand these basic truths about economics:

- ***Government-run markets don't work.*** Economics are natural forces that can't be managed politically without enabling corrupt politicians, hampering growth, and disrupting stability. In government-run economies, only a few individuals—usually dictators and their bureaucrats and military leaders—make the decisions for everybody else. Only the political elite are able to thrive;

everybody else is forced to accept the decisions of their rulers.

- **_Free markets work best._** The only proven way to increase prosperity and reduce poverty is through individual liberty, capitalism, and free markets. Free markets work because nothing happens unless *both* parties feel they can benefit. Businesses succeed only if they can get enough consumers to choose their products and services. *Both* the buyer and seller must agree on the price. *Both* the employee and employer must agree on the wage. Every individual makes his or her *own* choices. Nobody is forced to do anything. Free markets are efficient and democratic because they involve millions of people making millions of tiny buy-sell (or work-wages) decisions every day, with everybody making constant adjustments in response to market forces (supply and demand).

- **_Gentle adjustments_**. Free market economies make gentle adjustments every day based on millions of individual decisions by millions of consumers and investors. Everybody gets time to react to changing realities.

- **_Governments cause bubbles and painful crashes._** It's when politicians get involved that we experience painful cycles of boom and bust instead of the gradual daily adjustments of a free economy. Misguided politicians prolonged the Great Depression and caused the 2008 housing crash and financial crisis. The government does a lot of harm by trying to manage or stimulate the economy—often artificially prolonging boom periods—which only means that crashes hit harder and recoveries take more time. Yet politicians keep tinkering because *they* benefit themselves in the process and because too many unthinking voters say they want politicians to manage the economy, create jobs, and so on.

- **_Government guarantees and insurance are bad deals_**. Politicians love to use government guarantees because they don't show up in the budget. Citizens need to understand that government guarantees and government insurance are needed only for bad deals; otherwise somebody in the private sector would make the loan or insure the risk. If Fannie Mae and Freddie Mac didn't exist, banks would have a legitimate place to invest their money; they could make mortgage loans based on their merits and wouldn't have to spin them off to put the risk on somebody else.

- **_Government-fueled booms lead to big crashes_**. When political/government meddling (Fannie Mae and Freddy Mac) caused the artificial housing boom, Wall Street greed made it easy for people to borrow against the equity in their homes so they could live far beyond their means. This worked as long as the boom continued. When the inevitable housing crash came, the politicians bailed out the reckless bankers and Wall Street firms. Working people lost their homes, and taxpayers got stuck with the costs of the government bailouts.

- **_The law of unintended consequences_**. Government-imposed solutions usually backfire and hurt everybody. One good example is government price controls, which usually lead to shortages. Another example is minimum wage laws, which have increased the unemployment rate of young black males from less than 10 percent a generation ago to 30–40 percent now.

- **_Government economies invite political mischief_**. Government controls always create new opportunities for politicians to dish out political favors to friends and deny favors to others. That's how they make their money and attract contributions.

- **_People make their own smart decisions_**. We all make better decisions when we know we have the potential to benefit from our good decisions *and* suffer from the results of our bad ones. Nobody's decisions are as good when they are spending somebody else's money—which explains why home owners take better care of their property than renters and why bureaucrats and politicians make so many lousy decisions.

- **_Profits are good._** Many Americans have been brainwashed by media, educators, politicians, and bureaucrats to think *profit* is a dirty word. They need to think about how profits benefit all of us. First, profits are taxed, which reduces the tax burden on the rest of us. What's left is reinvested in creating new jobs; purchasing equipment; developing new, better, and less expensive products; or paid out as dividends to investors—including the retirement plans of millions of Americans. Yes, some of these dividends go to rich people, but they pay taxes first and then stimulate the economy even more by spending or investing what's left after taxes.

- **_Corporate taxes._** Higher corporate taxes can only come from three sources: higher prices for consumers, lower dividends for our pension plans, or the elimination of jobs. The key is to make sure corporate taxes (on the whole) are competitive globally so employers won't move more jobs to other countries.

- ***Creating jobs***. The government can't create additional jobs. When it takes money from others to create a government job, there's no net gain; it's usually a matter of turning a productive job in the private sector into a nonproductive and higher-cost government job (at taxpayer expense).

- ***Uncertainty hurts***. When politicians try to manage the economy and bureaucrats try to regulate it, they create economic uncertainty. As explained in the chapter titled "Taxes," investors and consumers hate uncertainty, so investment and consumption tend to stop, slow, or become volatile when politicians tinker with the economy. Uncertain tax policies and the uncertain costs of regulatory compliance often drive investors underground or overseas. Businesses hire when there is demand for their products and services. Banks lend when they can make enough money to justify the risk. When businesses fear higher taxes, more government mandates, and more government regulations, they stop investing and stop hiring. And when consumers fear for their own jobs, they reduce their spending.

- **_Government isn't free_**. As explained in the "Government" chapter, there is no such thing as a free government service. Government can only take some people's money and give it to others—and it does an inefficient job because its ever-expanding bureaucracies take so much off the top and then spend what's left poorly.

- **_Dividing the pie_**. The economic "pie" isn't a fixed amount that must be divided up fairly. Freeing the economy so the pie can grow (and benefit everybody) is the better approach. However, this shouldn't rule out the possibility of a safety net for the least fortunate among us, as explained in the chapter titled "Poverty."

- **_The global economy._** The shift to a global economy is particularly difficult for the United States because there's so much competition from third world countries that are leaner, hungrier, and sometimes even more creative than we are. Our overall standard of living is declining relative to the rest of the world, which is uncomfortable for us short-term but may be beneficial for humankind over the long haul.

How to fix
America's economics

> ➤ ***Education***. Voters need to understand basic economics. Once they do, they will stop asking politicians to fix the economy. (See the "Education" chapter for more about this.)

> ➤ ***Stop economic micromanagement.*** The government's first rule when it comes to the economy should be "first, do no harm." Politicians can't manage the economy, and bureaucratic efforts to control economics eventually backfire and do harm. No Congress or central planners can repeal the laws of supply and demand. Economies work best when millions of consumers are free to make their own individual decisions every day on a level playing field" with as little political interference and bureaucratic manipulation as possible.

> ➤ ***Phase out the Federal Reserve***. The money supply should be increased proportionate with actual economic growth; and interest rates and the value of the dollar should be determined by free markets rather than government manipulation.

> ➤ ***Get the government out of the insurance business***. Whenever the

government guarantees or insures anything, it's almost always because no sane person or business will take the risk. (See more about this point in the "Government" chapter.)

➤ ***Energy independence.*** As explained in the "Energy" chapter, we must relax some of the environmental regulations that prevent us from developing our own proven sources of energy. Doing this now would also be a powerful economic stimulus at a time when we desperately need one.

➤ ***Stability.*** Political uncertainty kills jobs. The best thing the government could do is create a favorable climate for economic growth by providing consistent and competitive taxes (as explained in the "Taxes" chapter) and regulation (as explained in the "Freedom" and "Government" chapters). Economic cycles will still occur, but they will correct themselves naturally and more gently. The painful periods of boom and bust that governments cause and prolong will be minimized.

➤ ***Stop welfare for businesses***. Phase out tax loopholes and government payments to businesses. (See the "Big Business" chapter for more details about this proposal.)

> ***Corporate governance reform.*** Stockholders should demand an end to the boardroom cronyism, interlocking directorships, and fat-cat consulting firms that allow management to rip off their companies at the expense of employees and shareholders. (Also see the "Big Business" chapter.)

> ***Negative income tax.*** The federal government should replace all its failing poverty programs with a brilliantly simple negative income tax. (See the "Poverty" chapter for more details about how the negative income tax would work.)

"The strongest argument for free enterprise is that it prevents anybody from having too much power. Whether that person is a government official, a trade union official, or a business executive, it forces them to put up or shut up. They either have to deliver the goods, produce something that people are willing to pay for, are willing to buy, or else they have to go into a different business." —American economist and author Milton Friedman

"Government's view of the economy could be summed up in a few short phrases: If it moves, tax it. If it keeps moving, regulate it. And if it stops moving, subsidize it." —Former U.S. President Ronald Reagan

"It was self-serving politicians who convinced recent generations of Americans that we could all stand in a circle with our hands in each other's pockets and somehow get rich." —American author and columnist Paul Harvey

"Inflation is not caused by the actions of private citizens, but by the government: by an artificial expansion of the money supply required to support deficit spending. No private embezzlers or bank robbers in history have ever plundered people's savings on a scale comparable to the plunder perpetrated by the fiscal policies of statist governments." —Ayn Rand, author, *Atlas Shrugged*

"DEMOCRAT: You have two cows. Your neighbor has none. You feel guilty for being successful. You push for higher taxes so the government can provide cows for everyone.
REPUBLICAN: You have two cows. Your neighbor has none. So?
SOCIALIST: You have two cows. The government takes one and gives it to your neighbor. You form a cooperative to tell him how to manage his cow.
COMMUNIST: You have two cows. The government seizes both and provides you with milk. You wait in line for hours to get it. It is expensive and sour.
CAPITALISM, AMERICAN STYLE: You have two cows. You sell one, buy a bull, and build a herd of cows.
BUREAUCRACY, AMERICAN STYLE: You have two cows. Under the new farm program, the government pays you to shoot one, milk the other, and then pour the milk down the drain.
AMERICAN CORPORATION: You have two cows. You sell one, lease it back to yourself and do an IPO on the 2nd one. You force the two cows to produce the milk of four cows. You are surprised when one cow drops dead. You spin an announcement to the analysts stating you have downsized

and are reducing expenses. Your stock goes up." —From the Internet, source unknown

"The preservation of freedom is the protective reason for limiting and decentralizing governmental power. But there is also a constructive reason. The great advances of civilization, whether in architecture or painting, in science or in literature, in industry or agriculture, have never come from centralized government." —Milton Friedman, author and economist

Fair Pay

"Far too many executives have become more concerned with the four P's—pay, perks, power, and prestige—rather than making profits for shareholders." —T. Boone Pickens, business tycoon

What's wrong about fair pay in America

- **_The income gap between rich and poor is growing_**. We'll always have rich and poor, but the gap between the two has been growing dangerously in America.

- **_Globalization hurts blue-collar workers._** As explained in the "Economics" chapter, the shift to a global economy is causing America's overall standard of living to decline relative to the rest of the world.

- **_Gains in productivity limit the number of jobs_**. To compete in a global economy, the United States has dramatically increased productivity—which is good. But most of these gains have come from finding ways to produce more with fewer workers (investments in more efficient equipment, technology, computers, and software) and from the massive outsourcing of jobs that can no longer be done for a competitive cost in the United States.

- ***For executives, bureaucracy trumps competition***. Competition is supposed to be the moderating force that determines each person's value in the workplace, but bureaucrats and their lobbyists have managed to suspend the rules, especially when Big Business, Big Labor, and Big Government are involved. So while blue-collar workers are suffering, the compensation of business and government leaders has become even more glaringly disproportionate.

- ***Crony compensation***. Big company executives pay consultants to recommend outlandish compensation plans. They pack their boardrooms with executive cronies who approve these plans. It's often a "you scratch my back and I'll scratch yours" arrangement. Then managers of labor unions and government agencies (where real competition is missing or limited) use comparisons to obscene corporate compensation to justify their own excessive compensation packages.

- ***Size matters***. Scale is part of the problem: when a company earns billions in profit, it may not seem unreasonable to pay the CEO a few million. When a professional sports league develops a virtual monopoly, it is perfectly natural for the owners, executives, coaches, and players to spat over who gets to divide a huge pie. And what government or union official doesn't want similar rewards for comparable duties?

- ***Long-term performance doesn't matter***. Most Americans don't resent it when brilliant executives earn a lot of money for creating real value. The trouble is that many Big Business executives reap obscene compensation for destroying value that somebody else created—very often by merging and slashing companies and laying off employees. The company may show impressive short-term profits, and the CEO can bail out with a golden parachute before the long-term damage becomes apparent.

- ***Government bailouts.*** When reckless behavior gets big businesses into trouble, politicians declare them "too big to fail" and use taxpayer money and credit to bail out the culprits. Then the companies reward their executives with obscene bonuses, and reward the politicians with more campaign contributions.

How to fix what's wrong with fair pay in America

> ➤ ***Government isn't the answer.*** Should the government step in to control the salaries of CEOs, Hollywood actors, and sports stars to make things fair? No. Over the long haul, free markets truly are the most efficient. The laws of economics simply cannot be legislated. Every time governments try to control wages or prices, they make a mess of it and people (usually those at the bottom of the economic ladder) get hurt. Government control also inevitably leads to more political corruption.

> ➤ ***Protectionism isn't the answer***. Can we use tariffs to protect American workers from the global economy? No. In fact, if politicians convince enough frustrated people that government control of the economy is needed to ensure fairness, we'll create a new generation of dependency and make it even less likely that we'll be able to thrive in the global economy.

> ➤ ***Freedom works.*** Free market competition is the best way to determine compensation levels. Make yourself more valuable, and you'll earn more. If your employer isn't willing to be pay you competitively, you can leave and go

elsewhere. Executives shouldn't be exempt from these principles.

➤ ***Executive compensation reform.*** Competition and disclosure are the keys to moderation. Instead of deferring to the recommendations of fat-cat consultants, corporate directors need to ask themselves if the company's executive compensation is truly competitive in the marketplace. (*"Would we really have to pay this much to attract a CEO as good as this one?"*) Along with other measurements, directors should consider any proposed compensation package as a multiple of the average worker's pay. (*"Is this executive really worth twenty-five times more than our average worker? Fifty times? One hundred times? Five hundred times?"*) Total executive compensation (not just salary) should be published in the annual reports of public companies. (See more about this in the "Big Business" chapter.)

➤ ***New skills for workers.*** American workers have always made whatever changes are needed—usually a lot faster than central planners expect, and in spite of burdens imposed on them by government bureaucrats, corporate executives, union leaders, and politicians. Now they'll figure out what skills are needed to thrive in a global economy. Many are thriving (even in a weak economy) because they have overcome their dependence on others and are reinventing themselves through individual initiative. In fact, these remarkable individuals (not big businesses) are driving the new economy in the United States (Also see the "Freedom" and "Education" chapters.)

> ➤ ***Safety net***. Some workers won't make the changes fast enough because they are too stuck in their old ways or too inclined to depend on a company, union, or government to take care of them. That's why we should adopt a negative income tax as a safety net and incentive to climb the ladder to prosperity. (See more about this in the "Poverty" chapter.)

"Democrats' definition of 'rich' always seems to be set just above whatever the salary happens to be for a member of Congress. Perhaps that says it all." —American entrepreneur Steve Steckler

"Hollywood is a place where they'll pay you a thousand dollars for a kiss and fifty cents for your soul." —American actor Marilyn Monroe

Poverty

"The tax that was supposed to soak the rich has instead soaked America. The beneficiary of the income tax has not been the poor, but big government. The income tax has given us a government bureaucracy that outnumbers the manufacturing work force. It has created welfare dependencies that have entrapped millions of Americans in an underclass that is forced to live a sordid existence of trading votes for government handouts." —Paul Craig Roberts

What's wrong with our poverty policies

- ***Our "War on Poverty" is a dismal failure***. In 1964, President Lyndon B. Johnson committed the nation to "cure" poverty. His intentions may have been good. But nearly 40 years later, the situation has only gotten worse --- with more people than ever dependent on government hand-outs.

- ***Political gridlock.*** All of us would prefer an ideal world with no poverty, but we all disagree—sometimes passionately—about how best to minimize poverty.

- **_Inefficiency_**. As explained in the "Government" chapter, the federal government doesn't do anything very well or very efficiently. For the war on poverty, it takes money out of the economy via taxation, ships it to Washington, spends a lot of it on inefficient bureaucracies, and then sends what's left back to other governments with so many mandates that even more money is wasted before anybody actually helps the poor.

- **_Costs are out of control._** The government claims there are forty-six million poor people in America. The Heritage Foundation estimates total federal and state government welfare spending at $714 billion. That's nearly $16,800 per year for each poor *person*. If you include people who receive welfare even though they aren't below the official poverty level, government spends $7,000 per year per person, or $28,000 annually for a family of four.

- **_Undermining families_**. The government's welfare programs encourage the wrong behaviors—such as avoiding marriage and giving birth to unwanted children in order to increase welfare amounts. When the War on Poverty started, 7 percent U.S. births were to unwed parents; today that number is 39 percent.

- **_Dependency_**. Government programs to help the poor often increase government dependency. These programs rob people of the self-respect that comes from achieving self-sufficiency, and they too often result in multiple generations of dependency, helplessness, and low self-esteem.

- **_Political dishonesty_**. Even one truly needy family living in poverty is too many, but governments tend to misrepresent the state of poverty in America in order to get more money for the bureaucrats who run poverty programs. Examples: Many Americans labeled by the government as living in *poverty* actually live in more comfort than the *average* family in many other countries. The federal census counts only four percent of total welfare spending as income. And the federal budget never counts welfare spending by the states even though most of spending by the states is mandated by the federal government.

- **_Government has stolen charity_**. American history is full of heartwarming stories about neighbors helping neighbors. Especially during the Great Depression, those stories included people sharing what little they had with complete strangers who were in even greater need. That spirit still survives, but it has been marginalized and subdued as government—using our tax money and our future credit—has become the biggest giver. What difference does the average citizen's $10 donation make if the government is giving $10 billion of our money to the same cause?

- ***Socialism doesn't work***. As discussed in the Economics" chapter, the only proven way to reduce poverty is to increase prosperity, and the only proven way to increase prosperity is through individual liberty, capitalism, and free markets. It's not a matter of dividing the pie "fairly"; it's a matter of growing it.

- ***Class warfare***. Career politicians and the special interest groups that control them have corrupted America's political and economic processes while giving lip service and false promises to the poor. The most unprincipled politicians put the nation's long-term future at risk by fanning the flames of class warfare.

How to fix poverty in America

> ***Phase out all federal welfare programs***. Since government has only made poverty more enduring, all government welfare programs and mandates should be phased out except tax deductions for charities and adoption of a negative income tax.

> ***A safety net***. Taking wealth from people who earned it to give to people who didn't earn it is like giving a person a fish instead of teaching him or her how to fish. It's self-defeating to consider the economic pie as something that must be divided up fairly; a much better approach is to free the economy so the pie can grow in ways that will benefit everybody. However, this shouldn't rule out the possibility of a safety net for the truly needy. A negative income tax would be the ideal safety net.

> ***Negative income tax***. The federal government should replace all its failing poverty programs with a brilliantly simple negative income tax as envisioned by the late libertarian economist Milton Friedman. This would give people a temporary "hand up" when they most need it, remove the stigma of being on welfare, provide incentives for people to pull themselves out of poverty and climb

the economic ladder, and eliminate the bureaucracy, waste, and fraud in the existing programs.

> ➤ **_How a negative income tax could work_**. Every adult and family would file a simple income tax return. Those earning under a minimum level (let's say, for example, $10,000 per adult or $20,000 per family) would receive cash (or a combination of cash and vouchers) to bring them up to the minimum; for every dollar earned, the subsidy would be reduced by fifty cents (so they would always have an *incentive* to earn more).

> ➤ **_Negative income tax examples._** Continuing with the example above, a family with $0 income would receive $20,000 in cash and vouchers, for a total income of $20,000. A family that earned $10,000 would receive $15,000, for a total income of $25,000; a family that earned $20,000 would receive $10,000, for a total income of $30,000; a family that earned $30,000 would receive $5,000, for a total income of $35,000; and a family that earned $40,000 or more would pay income taxes only on the amount over $40,000.

> ➤ **_Funding the negative income tax_**. Hundreds of welfare programs administered by federal, state, and local governments could be eliminated

entirely. The savings could determine the base income for the negative income tax and therefore entirely cover the cost of a negative income tax. The needy would actually get a lot more direct help than they do currently because the administrative overhead, waste, and fraud of the existing welfare programs would be eliminated. It would cost taxpayers no more in the short-term than is being spent currently—and it would cost less in the long-term because of the built-in incentives for people to work themselves up the economic ladder.

> ***What if recipients don't spend the money wisely?*** If some of the recipients prove incapable of managing the money wisely, vouchers for food and medical insurance could be substituted for some of the cash; the vouchers programs would best be administered at the state level.

> ***Marriage and unwanted babies.*** If the minimum income for single people is exactly half the amount for families, there would no longer be a financial incentive to avoid marriage. And if the minimum income for families is fixed regardless of family size, there would no longer be a financial incentive for poor people to have more children than they can afford. (If this creates a hardship for

some larger families, charities could step up to help.)

> ➤ ***Why federal?*** The reason for the negative income tax being federal is (as Willy Sutton used to say about robbing banks) "that's where the money is." As the federal government phases out its failing welfare programs and phases in a negative income tax, poverty would be dramatically reduced.

> ➤ ***Fighting poverty locally.*** Any remaining poverty issues (and there will always be some) could be dealt with by private individuals, religious organizations, foundations, and state and local governments. Individual charities and individual states—not the federal government—can best decide which programs are worthy, effective, and deserving of continued support. Imagine, for example, the potential of fifty different approaches to reducing poverty being tried by fifty different states.

> ➤ ***Ending poverty in America.*** The modest safety net provided by the negative income tax would assure that nobody would starve. Individuals who truly can't work due to family complications, physical problems, or mental issues would have their basic needs covered. This would eliminate any

excuses for poor people to turn to crime or beg in the streets. And everybody would still have an incentive to work if they are able.

> ***Work/school requirements?*** One way to administer the negative income tax would be for the federal government to send block grants to the states; then the individual states could determine whether its citizens should be required to work or get job training in order to qualify for the payments. It would take huge and expensive bureaucracies, however, to enforce a work/school requirement, and the bureaucrats would predictably do a lousy job of it. So, some states might choose to take a "no fault" approach, keep the safety net amount low enough that people will still have an incentive to work to better themselves, while counting on charities to take up the slack for those whose needs are greater.

> ***Avoid class warfare.*** The negative income tax would avoid the class warfare toward which the nation seems to be headed by creating a safety net for the poor and disabled while also giving poor people an incentive to climb the economic ladder.

> ***Reasons to support a negative income tax.*** Conservatives and liberals should

support the negative income tax because
it would give the needy a start up the
economic ladder—but without the
overlap, waste, and bureaucratic
overhead of hundreds of existing
government poverty programs.

"Welfare rights are pseudo-rights: They rely on the force of
law to take private property for the use of others without
compensation and without consent. Public charity is forced
charity; it is not a virtue but a vice." —Economics professor
and Cato Journal editor James A. Dorn

"Wealth is ultimately the only thing that can reduce poverty.
The most dramatic reductions in poverty, in countries around
the world, have come from increasing the amount of wealth,
rather than from a redistribution of existing wealth...And let
the rest of us exercise more judgment as to how much charity
is beneficial and how much more simply perpetuates
dependency, grievances and the polarization of
society."—American author and economist Thomas Sowell

"[T]he sprawl of government into every conceivable realm of
life has caused the withering of traditional institutions.
Fathers become unnecessary if the government provides Aid
to Families with Dependent Children. Church charities lose
their mission when the government provides food, shelter
and income to the poor. And the non-poor no longer feel
pressed to provide aid to those in need, be they aged parents
or their unfortunate neighbors—"compassion" having
become the province of the state." —American author and
columnist Mona Charen

Socialism

"The inherent vice of capitalism is the unequal sharing of the blessings. The inherent blessing of socialism is the equal sharing of misery." —Winston Churchill, former prime minister of Great Briton

"The difference between a welfare state and a totalitarian state is a matter of time." —Ayn Rand, author, *Atlas Shrugged*

What's wrong with Socialism

- ***Socialism doesn't work***. Central planning by government never works over the long haul, partly because individual initiative is crushed and individual responsibility is discouraged. The collapse of communism is a prime example. Today the declining economies in most of Europe provide further evidence. The United States is right behind them with our relentless shift toward socialism and our demands that government address every problem.

- ***More government means less freedom***. As discussed in the "Government" chapter, an all-encompassing government leaves less room for the individual initiative that made America great.

- ***Utopia or dictatorship***. Socialism describes an economic system in which the government controls wealth and professes to redistribute it fairly. Such an idea often attracts well-intentioned idealists who genuinely hope socialism will lead to a utopian society in which there is no hunger or suffering. It may sound good at first (especially to those who consider themselves to be victims), but socialism always leads to oppressive governments run by ruthless dictators.

- ***Individual serfdom***. Socialism leaves no room for individual decision making. The government's central planners control everything and make all of the decisions. They do this in the name of the people or the public good, but people become nothing more than small cogs in the government's grand scheme of things.

- ***Initiative dies***. With individual choices no longer tolerated, initiative dies. It then becomes a matter of the government—through its ruling class or dictator—"fairly" distributing the declining fruits of a failing economy to increasingly oppressed and dispirited citizens.

- ***Hunger and suffering***. Does socialism always lead to increasingly totalitarian governments that leave no room for individual liberty and to declining economies that produce even more hunger and suffering? Yes. Always. No exceptions. Don't take my word for this. Read some history, beginning with Friedrich A. Hayek's classic book, *The Road to Serfdom.*

How to reverse America's slide toward Socialism

> *__Individual liberty__*. To stop America's decline, we must recognize that the government can't take care of us—despite the promises of politicians when they run for office. (For more about this concept, see the chapter titled "Freedom.")

> *__Limited government__*. We must recognize that governments—especially big governments—don't do anything very well and often make matters even worse. (Also see the "Government" chapter.)

> *__Rein in the career politicians__*. Capping their pay and eliminating their special benefits and pensions would be good first steps. (See "Career Politicians" for more details about this proposal.)

> *__Free markets work best.__* As discussed in the "Economics" chapter, the only proven way to increase prosperity and reduce poverty is through individual liberty, capitalism, and free markets.

> *__A safety net__*. As explained in the "Poverty" chapter, a negative income tax would provide incentives for people to pull themselves out of poverty and climb the economic ladder, while also

eliminating the bureaucracy, waste, and fraud in existing federal, state, and local welfare programs.

"What is your fair share of what somebody else has earned?" —American columnist, economist, and author Thomas Sowell

"The problem with socialism is that eventually you run out of other people's money [to spend]."—British Prime Minister Margaret Thatcher

Take Back Congress

The common sense, brave hearts, and hard work of regular Americans made this country great.

Somehow we have allowed an elite political class—career politicians, their public relations experts, special interest lobbyists, central planners, bureaucrats, journalists, and a variety of other so called experts—to dominate political discourse in this country. These self-appointed experts have made a mess of it!

I still believe that regular citizens—like you and me—can do something about it. We can reclaim our government and restore America to a government "of, for, and by" the people. We should at least try, right? You can do your part by recommending this book to your family and friends and mentioning it during your social networking activities.

If citizens put enough pressure on them, politicians could be compelled to adopt reforms. If not, it may require four amendments to the Constitution, worded something like this:

1. ***Congressional compensation and term limits***. No individual may serve more than twelve years in the United States Congress. Congressional salaries may not exceed the median income of citizens. There shall be no pensions or benefits for

elected federal officials beyond Social Security and their own self-funded retirement accounts and insurance policies. Elected federal officials shall not accept any gift with a value exceeding $100, participate in initial public stock offerings or insider trading, or accept any government or government influence–related employment for at least four years after leaving office. (Also see the "Congressional Reform" chapter.)

2. *__Lobbyists, conflicts, and transparency.__* Any citizen or group that wishes to influence congressional legislation must submit their positions in writing. Any verbal communications with members of Congress about pending legislation must be followed by a confirming memo. With the exception of sensitive national security issues, transcripts of all congressional hearings shall be posted on the Internet for public access. All communications to members of Congress regarding specific legislation shall be posted on the Internet for public access at least twenty-four hours prior to congressional votes. Members of Congress shall be permitted to cast their votes electronically, so their physical presence in the nation's capital will no longer be necessary. (See the "Congressional Reform" chapter for more details.)

3. *__Campaign contributions__*. Candidates for elected federal offices shall accept campaign contributions only from individual citizens. Campaign contributions by businesses, political action committees, labor unions, trade associations, and other groups shall not be

permitted. All campaign contributions must be made a least one month prior to the applicable election, and full disclosure of the amount and source of each contribution shall be posted online at least two weeks prior to the election. (Also see the "Election Reform" chapter.)

4. ***Federal government overreach***. The Tenth Amendment to the US Constitution *("The powers not delegated to the United States by the Constitution, nor prohibited by it to the States, are reserved to the States respectively, or to the people.")* is reaffirmed, and Article I, Section 8, Clause 3 of the US Constitution *([The Congress shall have Power] "To regulate Commerce with foreign Nations, and among the several States, and with the Indian tribes")* is amended to delete these words: *"and among the several States."* (See the "Government" chapter for more information.)

All Constitutional amendments adopted thus far have been proposed by two-thirds of both houses of Congress and ratified by at least 75 percent of the states (once by state conventions; all others by state legislatures).

So the proven path would be for citizens to put enough pressure on Congress to start the process, and then put enough pressure on their state legislatures to ratify the amendments.

But if Congress won't propose amendments that would actually solve the problem, the Constitution provides two other ways for amendments to be adopted:

- Proposed by constitutional conventions in two-third of the states, and then ratified by 75 percent of the state constitutional conventions
- Proposed by constitutional conventions in two-thirds of the states, and then ratified by 75 percent of the state legislatures

Any of these approaches would be difficult. But if citizens become disgusted enough with America's broken politics, they can make it happen.

Action Plan

1. ***Restore freedom, power, and responsibility to citizens***. Citizens must start accepting responsibility for their families and for the consequences of their choices instead of expecting government to take care of them. Free people must have the freedom to succeed, as well as the freedom to fail. For more about what's wrong and how to fix it, see the "Citizens," "Civility," "Education", and "Individual Responsibility" chapters.

2. ***Take power back from the career politicians and the special interest groups that control them***. Eliminate all pensions for elected officials and cap their pay. Impose term limits, ban conflicts of interest, outlaw campaign contributions from special interest groups, and require full and timely disclosure of campaign contributions. Keep members of Congress out of Washington (where they're too tempted by lobbyists and too full of their own self-importance) and let them telecommute from home (where they'll do less harm, stay closer to taxpayers, and spend less taxpayer money on travel). For more about what's wrong and how to fix it, see the "Career Politicians," "Big

Business," "Big Labor," "Big Media,"
"Political Parties," "Election Reform,"
"Congressional Reform," and
"Censorship" chapters.

3. ***Stop burying citizens in hopelessly complex laws, regulations, and bureaucracies.*** Reaffirm separation of church and state, keep marriages separate from civil unions, and break the stalemates over abortions, gay rights, gun control, and health care. For more about what's wrong and how to fix it, see the "Freedom," "Bigotry," "Health Care," "Abortion," "Guns," and "Religion" chapters.

4. ***Limited but effective government.*** Insist that the federal government do a very few things very well instead of trying to do far too much and failing at almost everything. Consider fresh and practical solutions to our energy dependence, environmental concerns, and immigration policies. For more about what's wrong and how to fix it, see the "Government," "Energy & Environment," and "Immigration" chapters.

5. ***Fix what's clearly not working.*** Reclaim our financial liberty, restore fairness and simplicity to the tax laws, streamline the justice system, and stop burying citizens in government debt. Reform entitlements, stop deficit

spending, end the misguided war on drugs, stop capital punishment, and make prisoners earn their room and board. For more about what's wrong and how to fix it, see the "Deficits," "Crime, Courts & Prisons," "Entitlements," and "Taxes" chapters.

6. ***Inspire the rest of the world***. Set a good example for others with our freedom and economic success, not with bribes and military dominance. Promote individual liberty (not just "democracy") around the world. For more about what's wrong and how to fix it, see the "Democracy" and "National Security" chapters.

7. ***Tackle poverty and stop class warfare***. Help people rise from poverty to prosperity. Get the government off the back of America's economy. Replace our failing welfare programs with a brilliantly simple negative income tax to ensure that nobody will have to beg in the streets or turn to crime. For more about what's wrong and how to fix it, see the "Economics," "Fair Pay," "Poverty," and "Socialism" chapters.

Index

Index

**Page
227**

Index

Index

Index

Index

Index

Index

Testimonials

Here's what readers (all regular citizens, no career politicians) are saying about this book:

"I am so pleased that you have written this book! As citizens, we need to create a dialogue on all these issues. We can no longer leave it up to the politicians." —Nick H.

"I love this book. I want to shout 'hooray' on each page." —Dottie G.

"I admire your tight, clear, and friendly prose. You call them as you see them, but always succinctly, fairly, and without bombast; a great example of your own rules of civility. Your range of views, including many that aren't often found in the same place, is bound to encourage others to think outside their comfort zones too." —Jim B.

"Discussion groups could use this book to collectively (and constructively) talk about and come to grips with today's most important issues." —Bob R.

"Absolutely love your book! What really gets under my skin, are the people who are so blinded by ideology. The Bushies who thought W could no wrong and now the Obama lovers who think that if you don't like his policies, you don't like him because you are a racist." —Mike R.

"Congratulations! You have created an Epistle that actually updates and could have an appropriate subtitle: *The Federalist Papers II*. A lot of work. A lot of thought.

Great quotes. Madison and Hamilton would have been proud of you, as am I." —Fred N.

"Unfortunately, those who need to read this book will not. Much of what is proposed would require an act of Congress, so don't bet on it ever happening, even with demands from the general public!" —Andy W.

"It wouldn't be easy to amend the Constitution, but your proposed amendments might unite grassroots voters, AND Tea Party members, AND Occupy Wall Street supporters, AND state legislators—perhaps a critical mass that could make something happen if it already isn't too late." —Doug S.

"It was such a pleasure to read the most thorough and deep definition of the nation's problems that I have ever encountered." —Jim P.

"I agree with you almost 100 percent on just about everything. I urge you to give this book maximum exposure, although I fear our society has passed the point of no return in many ways." —Tom S.

"There's a lot of work and good thinking reflected in what you've written and I particularly like many of the quotes you chose to include. As a Conservative, I really like what you've said in the *'We can be choosy'* paragraph on Immigration and your position on deficits." —George H.

"I agree with everything you said in the 'Citizens' chapter except the statement that our generation has created this mess. I think our children started the 'me first' generation and they are passing it on to their children." —June A.

Made in the USA
Charleston, SC
23 April 2012